SYMBIOSIS

THE CURRICULUM AND THE CLASSROOM

KAT HOWARD AND CLAIRE HILL

First published 2020

by John Catt Educational Ltd,
15 Riduna Park, Station Road,
Melton, Woodbridge IP12 1QT

Tel: +44 (0) 1394 389850
Fax: +44 (0) 1394 386893
Email: enquiries@johncatt.com
Website: www.johncatt.com

ISBN: 978 1 913622 08 4

Set and designed by John Catt Educational Limited

REVIEWS

'A must read for schools who are considering their curriculum leadership structures – it outlines who should do what, and most importantly explores what happens if we get it wrong. It flies the flag for teacher agency and outlines the important role that subject leadership plays, teasing out how leaders can effectively support and quality assure the work of this powerhouse of middle leadership. Beautifully written, this book will adorn many a bookshelf of ambitious school leaders who want to ensure that curriculum work is at the heart of their school improvement strategy and that the subject expertise of teachers has high value – a sure-fire way to improve retention and aid recruitment.'

Helena Brothwell, Regional Director of David Ross Education Trust

'What a thoughtful, useful book. I'll be recommending this to headteachers and Trust executives and education leaders. As well as explaining underlying theory very lucidly, Kat Howard and Claire Hill have captured nuance and complexity, thus showing why leaders need to sustain conversation with subject detail, and support teachers in getting close to subject community discourse.'

Christine Counsell, education consultant,
previously senior lecturer at the University of Cambridge
and Director of Education of a Multi-Academy Trust

'This book interweaves experience, expertise, and a host of different theoretical positions to form a notable contribution across primary and secondary education. This book will provide a powerful critical reflection for teachers as they tackle the design and delivery of curriculum within their settings.

The authors present a clear position on what they believe should drive curriculum, without creating false binaries or stoking the flames of controversy. The authors are calm, nuanced, yet strong. Over the course of the book, they gently invite the reader to reflect and consider their position. Furthermore, they provide informed, take-away action points for the convinced and ready to act.

A stimulating read on curriculum that's a great resource for the thinking, reflective teacher.'

Professor Neil Gilbride,
Lecturer in Education, University of Gloucester

'So often the curriculum is positioned as a rarefied entity, separate from the classroom and the lived experience of teachers and students. This book seeks to reposition the curriculum as something at the heart of everyday school life and offers clear guidance to school leaders and teachers based on solid evidence. This book is indispensable for anyone thinking about what we should be teaching today.'

Dr Carl Hendrick, author of *How Learning Happens*

'A sign of a really good book is when I read it once and then want to immediately return to a section again – I've read this book through once, and then returned to several sections two or three times. Claire and Kat have combined a comprehensive body of research alongside practical strategies that can be used by curriculum leaders at all levels. Not only does it put curriculum at the forefront of the reader's thinking, but it also ensures this is achieved while keeping teachers' AND leaders' workload in mind.

The model this book offers for designing and implementing a collegiately created curriculum is excellent and will help chart the journey of curriculum for many schools. I will be purchasing and using sections of this book with my curriculum leaders to help me get new and novice curriculum leaders up to speed; I'm looking forward to sharing it with my team!

This really is a book for qualification reading lists. Seriously impressive stuff.'

Nimish Lad, Vice Principal and science teacher

'If you are looking to improve your school's curriculum in light of the work of great curricular thinkers such as Michael Young and Christine Counsell then you must read this brilliant book. *Symbiosis* is a tour-de-force of deep curricular thinking, providing substantial insight into the thought processes of designing a rich, coherent curriculum.'

Andrew Percival, Primary Deputy Head

'Before you read this book, please make sure you are adequately equipped. You will, at the very least, need a pencil, sticky-notes, a note pad, a highlighter, a photocopier, your laptop and your mobile phone within reach. If you fail to heed this friendly advice, I promise you won't get past page 9 before you jump up and demand, 'for the love of God, someone get me a sticky-note!'.

You can't just read *Symbiosis*. Instead, you are compelled to have a complete interactive experience with it. It's the kind of book where not a page goes by where you don't think, 'I must share that with my team' or 'this whole page needs photocopying for my office wall', or 'that is a great quote – I must share it right now.'

The curriculum debate we're having in education right now is focused on subject-specificity, so a whole book on curriculum runs the risk of being generic. This book, however, is anything but generic. On the contrary, it cleverly explores the substance of the curriculum by demonstrating, through many practical examples, how curriculum thinking manifests itself in the classroom. In many ways, it is an essential handbook for the classroom. I will definitely be recommending it to all my teachers.

It's also a book about leadership, which is curious, because it makes no claim on leadership. It explores the way that senior and middle leaders can ask questions about the relationship between the curriculum and the classroom, but it's very definitely not purporting to be a book about 'leadership'. And yet, I feel I learned more about leadership in reading this book than I have about innumerable titles that approach leadership generically.

Overall, this is a triumph of a book: a book which positions curriculum as the 'what' and the classroom as the site of 'how', which preserves the dignity of the curriculum whilst practically advising how it should become manifest in the classroom. It's also a book about professional development, teacher workload, autonomy, candid relationships and school culture. Finally, it's a book about what unites, not divides us – which is needed in education now more than ever.'

Carly Waterman, Secondary Principal, founding member of Educating Northants

For Austen

For Ben, Noah, Ted and Max

CONTENTS

FOREWORD

Greater attention to the curriculum across the sector is a very good thing. Driven in part by the quality of education judgement in the Education Inspection Framework (2019),[1] curriculum conversations are alive and full of healthy debate about the purpose, implementation and impact of what is provided for pupils in our classrooms.

What has been missing, however, is an articulation of how the headlines are translated to the classroom. In other words, the thread of accountability for a high-quality curriculum from senior leaders to curriculum leaders to teachers. *Symbiosis* addresses this gap. Written by two thinkers who are both leaders and teachers, *Symbiosis* is the first book to breathe life into the journey from theory to practice. It points out the disconnection, evident in many parts of the sector, of a leadership-led, top-down model of curriculum enactment where agency stops at the top. Claire Hill and Kat Howard argue, correctly, that in order for the curriculum to land deliberately in the classroom, it requires the active involvement of all involved in the business of teaching. To neglect to involve teachers in this work is to 'risk undermining staff members' sense of feeling trusted and their own intrinsic motivation, potentially leading to disengagement, burnout and leaving.[2] They make the case for a strong, irrefutable line of curriculum obligations at all levels.

The first section of the book tackles the role of senior leaders in setting the scene for curriculum development. It points out the problems of 'lethal

---

1. Education Inspection Framework, accessed at https://www.gov.uk/government/publications/education-inspection-framework , July 2020
2. Worth, J. and Van den Brande, J. (2020) *Teacher Autonomy: how does it relate to job satisfaction and retention?* Slough: NFER.

mutations' and the importance of doing fewer things, well. It recognises that curriculum is a demanding but worthwhile endeavour, and acknowledges that there are no silver bullets (or their close relation – quick fixes). It also pursues the logic of defining what professional development looks like when priorities are shifted to serious curriculum development. As Kennedy argues, 'from the teachers' perspective, the education system is "noisy".[3] We need to strip things back, to encourage professional curiosity and careful, focused feedback that does not 'distract teachers from the main objective or message on which we wish to focus our energies.[4]

At the subject leadership level, Hill and Howard provide a roadmap for getting to the heart of the matter: the articulation of the value of the subject; the entitlement of powerful knowledge for every child; the importance of concepts in sequencing and in providing the 'holding baskets' for lots of knowledge; how to address the subject in a scholarly way; the history and heritage of individual subjects; the importance of the hinterland; and the significance of substantive, disciplinary, declarative and procedural knowledge. Importantly, they outline the oft-hidden problem of 'fragile' knowledge. These insights are a goldmine for subject leaders who are engaged in this work, and provide a new lens and vocabulary through which to refine their thinking.

For the teacher enacting the curriculum in the classroom – many of whom will also be subject and senior leaders – the key aim should be a quest for elegance in the implementation of the curriculum through 'careful thinking around structure, substance and simplicity', so that we provide an enriching and meaningful enactment of the curriculum for both teachers and students.

There are insights into the importance of teacher autonomy, of crafting great enquiry questions, and of anticipating misconceptions. This is

3.   Kennedy, M. (2016) 'How does professional development improve teaching?', *Review of Educational Research*, 86 (4), 10.3102/0034654315626800.
4.   Wilkins, R. (2011) *Research Engagement for School Development*. London: Institute of Education.

amplified with findings from cognitive science that help us to help pupils learn more deeply and more meaningfully. There are very significant insights into workbooks, which help teachers identify where their time is best directed in the lesson and in their own development of subject knowledge. The aim is to extricate teachers from cutting, pasting and formatting hefty one-use PowerPoints so they are liberated to spend time working collaboratively with others to discuss, review, evaluate and refine their delivery of the material itself rather than the making of it. As Russell Hobby says, 'the job of a good curriculum is to inspire teachers, not instruct them.'[5]

We might have all the ingredients for a great curriculum, but it requires meaningful professional development for it to be effectively implemented. The work of professional development is the subtlest of arts: at its heart should be the assumption that people want to refine their craft, and they want to get better. This is in contrast to a deficit model that assumes colleagues need sticks and carrots. In *Symbiosis*, Hill and Howard articulate the balance between accountability (the notion that we expect to be accountable for our work) and trust (which assumes that professionals do not need to be micro-managed) to arrive at a system which focuses on curriculum development as teacher development. When this is in place, powerful curriculum development is the driver for professional development. As Vivienne Robinson has identified, 'problem-solving is a largely social process, and it requires leaders at all levels to have high ability in the third capability, that of building relational trust.'[6]

Crucially, this book is much more than a factual guide to the curriculum in schools. Their articulation of 'the wicked problem of the curriculum' is driven by a moral purpose, by two practitioners who walk the talk. It is inspiring and helpful in equal measure and will make a significant

5.   Interview with Russell Hobby, Cambridge Assessment, 6th November 2013.
6.   Robinson, V. M. J. (2019) 'Excellence in educational leadership: practices, capabilities and virtues that foster improved student outcomes', in T. Bush, L. Bell and D. Middlewood, *Principles of Educational Leadership and Management*. London: Sage Publications.

ACKNOWLEDGEMENTS

Thank you to all those that took the time to share their wisdom:

David Alderson, Dr Morvan Barnes, Tom Bennett,
Elisabeth Bowling, Helena Brothwell, Andy Buck,
Dominic Burrell, Louise Cass, Christine Counsell,
Sarah Donarski, David Didau, Drew End,
Dr Neil Gilbride, Tarjinder Gill, Josh Goodrich,
Angel Grantham, Dr Carl Hendrick, Michelle Jones,
Joanne Jukes, Nimish Lad, Louise Lewis,
Peter Mattock, Amanda McKenzie, Kathryn Morgan,
Kate O'Hara, Charley O'Regan, Anna Reynard,
Laura May Rowlands Michelle Shepherd, Tom Sherrington,
Samuel Strickland, Jack Tavassoly-Marsh, Joanne Tiplady,
Carly Waterman, Gary Wootton, Krissy Yates,

INTRODUCTION
THE ROLE OF THE CURRICULUM

Curriculum is not a component of education: it *is* education. Start a discourse in your school, in any school, and it will lead you back to the thought, design and direction of the curriculum. It acts to inform every decision we make, at every level, to ensure that the intention and purpose of schools remains clear. As Martin Robinson states, 'the main job of a school isn't to help pupils get high grades, it is to help provide meaning. This is the function of curriculum.'[7] Of course, national assessments are essential and unavoidable – they are our students' ticket to whatever comes next. John Tomsett goes further and argues that 'the best pastoral care for students from the most deprived backgrounds is a great set of exam results.'[8] However, it is our curriculum that enables us to provide just that. It is our cornerstone; whether this is due to its function or its beauty, our decisions now have curriculum at their heart. This more explicit focus on curriculum is promising, but we need to ensure we are well-equipped to tackle the task at hand.

Curriculum and moral purpose

Our focus on curriculum goes beyond just being part of the work of schools. As Sarah Hubbard affirms, it is 'an important lever for social justice.'[9] By not taking care over our curriculum thinking, possibilities and opportunities can remain hidden from students; our curriculum needs to make these visible. Here, Amanda Spielman illustrates the precarious nature of poor curriculum experience:

---

7. Robinson, M. (2013) *Trivium*. Independent Thinking Press.
8. Tomsett, J. (2015) 'Data is the key to educating the whole child'. Schools Improvement, https://schoolsimprovement.net/john-tomsett-data-is-key-to-educating-the-whole-child/.
9. Sarah Hubbard at The Team English National Conference, 4 July 2020.

Children can go all the way through secondary school and then go bump when they hit real demands in post-16 education or have aspirations for university, because they just don't have the experience or practice of reading more demanding texts. Schools can think they are being helpful by adapting and providing relevant material. But in fact it hollows out education and means that disadvantaged children don't get the experience that they absolutely should. The job of schools is to make sure that children get the things they won't necessarily get at home.[10]

Whilst we cannot present curriculum as a panacea to resolve all social ills, it is the finest instrument we have to ensure the children in our care receive a rich, coherent and ambitious education that takes them beyond their own experiences so they can confidently meet the demands of whatever comes next. Our role is to ensure that when they reach adulthood and join society, they feel like a participant and not a spectator.

When faced with such an important task, it becomes necessary to reframe our systems, processes and lines of inquiry to ensure our curricular work is given the time and status it requires. We not only need to demonstrate what successful work on the curriculum looks like, we need to put in place the mechanisms required to support such work. Creating systems and opportunities that offer 'a secure focus on pedagogical and subject knowledge,'[11] and promoting and encouraging 'teachers' belief that teaching is worthwhile,'[12] is sorely required for us to be successful.

10. Savage, M. (2018) '"Schools give poor pupils easier texts"': Ofsted head's list of areas to improve', *The Guardian*, 15th September 2018, accessed at https://www.theguardian.com/education/2018/sep/15/schools-give-poor-pupils-easier-texts-ofsted-heads-list-of-areas-to-improve on 15th May 2020.

11. Cruddas, L. (2016) 'Recruiting and Retaining Teachers – the Art of the Possible', in J. Simons (ed.), *The Importance of Teachers: a collection of essays on teacher recruitment and retention.* Policy Exchange.

12. Ofsted (2019), *Summary and recommendations: teacher well-being research report,* accessed at https://www.gov.uk/government/publications/teacher-well-being-at-work-in-schools-and-further-education-providers/summary-and-recommendations-teacher-well-being-research-report.

The detachment of the curriculum from the classroom

There can sometimes be a detachment between curriculum as an entity within schools and the way teachers feel engaged and purposeful in what they do in the classroom. To neglect to involve teachers in this curricular work is to 'risk undermining staff members' sense of feeling trusted and their own intrinsic motivation, potentially leading to disengagement, burnout and leaving.'[13] To attempt to solve the wicked problem of curriculum we need to consider how a teacher's relationship with the curriculum and their engagement with the profession are inextricably linked. When the curriculum is prepared by senior leaders or external providers, independent of those in the classroom, not only can teachers feel excluded from the aspects of their role that offer fulfillment and purpose, but the development of their teaching practice is also limited as this development is inextricably linked to our relationship with the curriculum.

Rather than look for silver bullets, mistaken that this will pacify issues of workload, we can look to study the curriculum thoughts of others to inform our own approach and bring richness and debate to our own conception and understanding. Rather than the curriculum being an add-on, a distraction, a problem in need of a quick fix, we need to recognise the work of the curriculum as exactly what can revitalise the sense of satisfaction, fulfilment and meaning of teaching itself.

Communication and connection

It is vital that our role as teacher, expert and curriculum curator is not lost in translation. Christine Counsell states:

> Your very being as a teacher from the word go should be thinking about what you're teaching. And if you're not thinking about what you're teaching, then you can't be teaching well – you're just a conduit. Being involved in big curricular choices

---

13. Worth, J. and Van den Brande, J. (2020) *Teacher autonomy: how does it relate to job satisfaction and retention?* Slough: NFER.

about flow, direction or angle, all affects how micro teaching moves, such as emphasis, passion or where to indicate mystery. How you package, how you shape it, how you really uncover and unpack a subject for children is fundamental.[14]

As experts of our subject, we look to become experts of curriculum. Only, this is not always the direction we are pointed towards. Instead, we can become experts of Excel spreadsheets, experts in reprographics, or experts in reading mark schemes: all of which redirect our efforts and attention away from 'keep[ing] the main thing the main thing.'[15] If we are to instead become experts of curriculum, this needs to be at the centre of what we do in schools.

It is with this leading principle that we look to how the curriculum is designed, communicated and delivered: from whole-school rationale, to collegiality within and between subjects, to being placed into the hands of the teacher to pass on to the student. The theory and thinking behind the curriculum is only as effective as its shape and form in the day-to-day operation of the classroom – it relies upon communication and interpretation at every level to ensure the inclusion of all owners and participants. We cannot just talk about what good curriculum design looks like: we have to live it.

A collaborative effort is also crucial to how we endure as a profession: the connection that we experience to the curriculum is what determines the longevity of our careers. A disconnection between the design and rationale of the curriculum and our role in its delivery acts to disempower and de-professionalise teachers, undermining their expertise and ultimately diminishing their sense of purpose. Curriculum work must therefore be 'done with' teachers and not 'done to'. The curriculum cannot be 'owned' by one person and delivered by another, and we cannot extricate

---

14.   Interview with Katherine Howard and Christine Counsell, 2019.
15.   Covey, S. (2004, 15th ed.) *The 7 Habits of Highly Effective People: Powerful Lessons in Personal Change.* The Free Press.

the curriculum from what happens in the classroom – *this relationship is symbiotic.* As warned against by Young,[16] if curriculum becomes simply a 'transmission of knowledge' we risk 'treat[ing] the knowledge that makes up the curriculum of the subject as inert', thereby failing to 'develop a relationship with knowledge' for both teachers and students. We therefore need to create the conditions required for all to participate in this important work.

Symbiosis: the curriculum and the classroom

With the contention that the relationship between the curriculum and the classroom is symbiotic, this book considers the role that everyone plays in curriculum development and why this is vital to the quality of education both now and in the future. It is challenging to involve all in this work, but it is necessary. Senior leaders, leaders of the subject, the classroom teacher – all have a professional duty to the curriculum. To confidently articulate why something is present, excluded, modified or wrangled with is an aim for all, because as curriculum designers and participators, this is our purpose.

The chapters that follow offer a framework for curriculum development at every stage, outlining the role of the senior leader, subject leader and classroom teacher in shaping the curriculum for our students. The first section addresses how senior leaders can create the conditions for meaningful curricular work, and looks at how we may reconfigure the role of 'senior leader' into 'curriculum leader' to ensure that this work is successful. The section that follows provides subject leaders with a road map for investigating the subject discipline in a way that is loyal to its complexities and nuances, exploring the considerations required when translating this from curriculum model to classroom practice. The third section focuses on implementation in the classroom, drawing together cognitive science and pedagogical theory to help move the curriculum from abstract design to practical delivery. The final section addresses how

---

16. Young. M, 'From Powerful Knowledge to the Powers of Knowledge', in C. Sealy & T. Bennet (eds.), *The researchED Guide to the Curriculum.* John Catt.

we can support teachers at all levels, bringing professional development firmly in line with curriculum development to ensure our curricular work is purposeful and not lost in translation.

This book follows a thread from whole-school decisions for the curriculum to the considerations of the subject leader to the daily minutiae of classroom instruction, to illustrate how this immutable thread connects us to the curriculum and to our sense of purpose as teachers.

SECTION ONE: WHOLE SCHOOL
CREATING THE CONDITIONS FOR CURRICULUM DEVELOPMENT

For a long time, the word 'curriculum' referred to how many lessons were allocated on the timetable. It has since taken on a very different meaning due to more rigorous exam requirements and a new Ofsted framework which looks to explore 'what is on offer, to whom and when [alongside] leaders' understanding of curriculum intent and sequencing, and why these choices were made'.[17] Where curriculum may before have been the domain almost entirely of the subject leader or classroom teacher, senior leaders are now often required to have a far more discerning knowledge of the curriculum offer in every subject. This section outlines the challenges of curriculum development and how to navigate these, alongside questions and considerations that look to reframe the role of senior leader as curriculum leader to help create the desired conditions for meaningful curricular work to take place.

17.   Ofsted (2019), *Inspecting the curriculum: revising inspection methodology to support the education inspection*, https://assets.publishing.service.gov.uk/government/uploads/system/uploads/attachment_data/file/814685/Inspecting_the_curriculum.pdf.

CHAPTER 1
SENIOR LEADERS AS
CURRICULUM LEADERS

There is now a need for senior leaders to have a more insightful understanding of subject disciplines outside of their own; a need for subject leaders to articulate the what and why of their curriculum design; a need for a clear understanding of the curriculum as a model for progression; and a need for a wider overview of the relationship between subjects as interconnected components. The implications of this can be overwhelming, as the time, training and investment required to achieve these aims can seem entirely insurmountable. On top of that, as a senior leader, how do you ensure you have the knowledge and skill to undertake meaningful discourse with a multitude of subjects – their heritage, progression, conceptualisation and evolution – so that you are in a position to determine such quality?

Lethal mutations

To remedy such contentions, we sometimes look for quick fixes, creating knowledge organisers and curriculum posters, completing generic checklists for schemes of work and writing intent statements. This is married with a culture of accountability whereby quantifiability is favoured over effectiveness. To attempt to measure and quantify the unwieldy beast that is whole-school curriculum, we find things we can measure: grades from lesson observations, data tracking, references to literacy, numeracy and 'cultural capital', or even the number of retrieval practice questions per lesson. Many of these approaches begin with good intentions and, in some cases, a good evidence-base.

Unfortunately, as is so often the case, potentially good ideas suffer from 'lethal mutations'[18] caused by a lack of training, investment, opportunity and evaluation. A CPD session that introduces the 'desirable difficulties'[19] of spaced practice and contextual interference may be grounded in cognitive research, but when hurriedly applied in practice may result in departments erratically sequencing the teaching of content in the hope of achieving improved outcomes, with the result likely to be quite the opposite. Or it may be that research is shared that correlates academic oracy with examination outcomes, and so follows a whole-school day of lessons without pens in students' hands, forcing departments to manipulate their curriculum plans for one-off, throwaway lessons to fit these new initiatives. These poor proxies for curriculum quality detract from and take time away from the more complex but more effective ways we can develop the curriculum. They leave staff feeling not only a lack of direction, but a deep sense of dissatisfaction – the work seems lacking in substance or utility, because it is not representative of their subject.

Do less, better

The approaches that are most likely to be effective in the long term are eminently more difficult to both quantify and to deliver. Supporting teachers' development of subject knowledge; time and training given for effective collaborative planning; introducing iterative, instructional coaching; and investing in high-quality, personalised teacher development – these all support the implementation of a coherent, well-designed, well-delivered curriculum. However, they are all difficult to quantify and require time and training to do well, so are less likely to be central to school systems. Yet if we agree that the curriculum is central to the quality of education, we have to look at how we can make this investment and how we make it worthwhile.

If we know that developing and delivering an effective curriculum requires time and investment, then we need to rigorously evaluate our use of time

18. Wiliam, D. (2011) *Embedded Formative Assessment*. Solution Tree Press.
19. Bjork, R. A. (1994) 'Memory and metamemory considerations in the training of human beings', in J. Metcalfe & A. Shimamura (eds.), *Metacognition: knowing about knowing*. Cambridge, MA: MIT Press.

in schools and strip away anything we are doing that does not contribute to these aims. We need to be mercenary when it comes to opportunity cost. If we want initiatives to be effective, something else we are doing needs to be taken away.

In its 2010 review of the national strategies, Ofsted found that 'typically, schools had several initiatives underway simultaneously. This often made it difficult to evaluate which ones were making a positive difference and which were not, as exemplified by a local authority consultant who said: "We often have to move to a new initiative before we know the impact of those we have just worked on."[20] This approach can increase workload exponentially without any evidence that the time and energy being spent on any one initiative is effective.

Like the national strategies that came before, we run this risk again with our current focus on curriculum development. Far better then to do fewer things well and evaluate, refine and develop these over time than to overload and overwhelm with initiatives that we have no way of knowing have had their desired effect. We need to be forensic in ensuring our focus and efforts are steadfastly invested in what will genuinely improve our curriculum and outcomes, and not be distracted by the promise of new initiatives in the hope that something might stick.

To assist our evaluation, approaches and policies should always pass two tests:

1. **Is this likely to directly improve the education of the student?**
2. **Is this the most efficient approach in terms of staff workload?**

It is not enough for any policy to pass only one of these tests. When strategies are then implemented, these need time to embed and to start making an impact. We need to ensure we have effective systems of

---

20. Ofsted (2010) *The national strategies: a review of impact,* https://dera.ioe.ac.uk/1102/1/The%20 National%20Strategies%20a%20review%20of%20impact.pdf.

evaluation and monitoring in place to ensure they are having their desired effect. Again, we can look to Ofsted's national strategies impact report, where it was found that a lack of effective evaluation led to 'too much monitoring that yielded little new information [...] simplistic measures of impact [...] pressure to evaluate initiatives too early [and] multiple requests for the same information.'[21] The result of this was a quality assurance system which lacked rigour and suffered from an absence of incisive action planning due to a lack of robust evaluation.

Ineffective methods of evaluation cause a lack of direction, with misdirected goals. What then proceeds from this is an increase in workload with very little impact, eventually resulting in another good idea being resigned to the educational recycling pile.

Measuring the unmeasurable

As we look to measure the impact of what we do, and attempt to work out exactly what it is that will give us an accurate indicator of success, we find ourselves as teachers turning to data analysis – and data analysts we are not. Consequently, we reach for measurements that will provide us with neat tables, graphs or spreadsheets, colour coded and ready to translate. We attempt to solve the unsolvable with the tools available to us, and they are rarely fit for purpose. We can at times be left with a tangle of data that diminishes the purpose of the curriculum itself, trying to present rich knowledge as tick boxes and competency checks.

Our subjects, and indeed our staff, are capable of far more than this, but because we are unable to present this richness and complexity in a linear format, we sacrifice the needs of the subject, staff and students at the altar of the data gods. This misguided approach leads to a number of undesirable outcomes, whether in making inaccurate judgements regarding student progress, writing assessments and mark schemes that are not fit for purpose, changing our curriculum without merit, or misidentifying students that most need our help. Our curriculum cannot

---

21.   Ibid.

compete with a system that does not reflect or value its intricacies and complexities and instead looks to measure and confine. The irony being, if we focus on curriculum and assess and respond to the level of mastery achieved at each stage of teaching, we get a better curriculum and better data. As Fordham proposes: 'the curriculum *is* the progression model.'[22]

Rejecting genericism

Whilst senior leaders have a view of wider school policy, this overarching view needs to be sympathetic to individual subject disciplines. School improvement is often unsuccessful when policies ask subjects to comply with generic strategies that mangle and manipulate the discipline. This approach removes the 'dignity of the thing'[23] by attempting to appropriate 'what works' in one subject and applying it to all.

We all benefit from seeing good models but these need to take account of the distinct differences between subjects and that the best way to design and deliver the curriculum for one subject is likely to differ from another. We will not master key concepts in mathematics without formula; we will only dilute our specialism in English if we try to employ the same method. Equally, if we attempt to constrain the curriculum to a cross-subject scheme of work template, we risk paying disservice to a subject through our attempt to bend and manipulate it to fit into neat tables and boxes. Streamlining subjects down to 'one size fits all' is naive to both the subject and those who serve it; the curriculum cannot be tamed in this way.

In the same vein, we cannot hope to measure our curricular success through exam performance alone. As Amanda Spielman affirms, the measure of success for our schools is 'not the exam grades or the progress scores, important though they are, but instead the real meat of what is taught in our schools and colleges: the curriculum.'[24] The way we measure

---

22. Fordham, M. (2020) 'What did I mean by "the curriculum is the progression model?"', https://clioetcetera.com/2020/02/08/what-did-i-mean-by-the-curriculum-is-the-progression-model/.

23. Counsell, C. (2020) 'The dignity of the thing', https://thedignityofthethingblog.wordpress.com/.

24. Spielman, A. quoted in Murray, C. (2017) 'How schools can develop a strong curriculum', https://schoolsweek.co.uk/how-schools-can-develop-a-strong-curriculum/.

success needs to be reframed as something fit for purpose: a methodology that recognises that curriculum must be designed, undertaken, delivered and evaluated with a sensitive touch – bespoke to the subject itself.

If we are to avoid genericism, then trust in the design and delivery of curriculum rests in the hands of subject leaders. We therefore need to create the conditions for subject leaders to do this effectively. If we start by stripping back anything that does not support this, we are left with what does. However, we need to be explicit in how this is communicated. When we ask a teacher or subject leader to spend time inputting data, answering emails or creating spreadsheets, then we are communicating that those aspects of their role are what is important. Our actions reinforce that this is our priority, even if we do so whilst simultaneously claiming that curriculum is king.

The system relies on ensuring that teacher perception aligns with what we set out to achieve: if curriculum *is* king, then all other tasks cannot be as well. As school leaders, our repeated messages and actions determine how teachers will interpret what is important, valued, rewarded, and what is not. If we do not ring-fence time to develop curriculum then it becomes an afterthought, an addition. We need to communicate the importance placed on curriculum through not just writing it down or saying it aloud to staff, but by our actions. We need to incubate teacher time that can be spent on curriculum development by reducing time spent on data drops, spreadsheets and laborious marking policies.

If there is agreement that the curriculum model is the progression model, and we ensure that our policies meet the two tests of impact and workload, then it is possible to refocus energies into designing an effective curriculum. Senior leaders therefore have a responsibility to articulate that curriculum is where teacher energy is most effectively invested by ensuring the support mechanisms are there to enable them to do so.

Questions and considerations

The following questions aim to support senior leaders in creating the conditions for effective curricular work to take place.

What will be reduced or removed from your policies and procedures to allow staff to focus their time and attention on the curriculum?[25]

- Consider what in your policies can be made more efficient, whether that's data input, feedback policies, or use of meeting time.

- Consider the opportunity cost of all of your school practices and weigh up their impact with the workload they create – if they do not pass the two tests of having high impact and reducing workload, something needs to change.

- Speak to staff and ask which tasks or aspects of their role they feel inordinately affect their workload and/or seem ineffective or lacking in impact. This may be a case of perception and leaders therefore need to better communicate the use or purpose of these tasks. Alternatively, this may help leaders evaluate the necessity of these tasks and their opportunity cost.

- Evaluate the allocation of duties to different roles. For example, are subject leaders spending too much time on administrative tasks or data analysis that could be completed by a central team to free up time to focus on curriculum? Ultimately, several people within a school are able to complete administrative and data roles; only subject leaders and their teams can design and implement their curriculum.

---

25. An effective mechanism for this is Andy Buck's 'MICK review', whereby staff are asked what they should do 'More' of, along with what they should look to 'Include', 'Change' or 'Kick out'.

How will CPD be designed to focus on the needs of teachers and subject leaders in supporting their development of the curriculum?

- Through an evaluation of the CPD needs of staff via audits and line management conversations, identify where gaps in staff knowledge and expertise need to be addressed.

- Direct teachers and subject leaders towards high-quality subject communities.

- Ensure CPD such as INSET days are well balanced, with regular focus on subject enhancement and development alongside teaching and learning practices.

- Ensure that where models of good practice are shared as part of CPD, the examples are applicable to different subjects without mangling their subject disciplines: where can subjects learn from one another in a way that is useful, purposeful and applicable whilst being sensitive to their distinct disciplines?

- Devise CPD programmes to offer staff personalised training based on their needs. For example, an NQT may require different input to an experienced teacher. However, training should not be divided along lines of experience – which is where audits are required to provide further insight of the expertise of your teams.

How will CPD and directed time be organised to support collaborative planning, instructional coaching and subject-focused curriculum conversations?

- Consider the use of directed time over a year and how much of this is given to subject-focused CPD and collaborative planning. Plan how this time will be used effectively over the course of the year ahead.

- Ensure staff are trained in how to collaboratively plan. Be explicit about why it is an important part of teaching and curriculum planning, and explicitly model this to help ensure time spent collaboratively planning is used effectively. In one-person departments, address how they will be supported by subject communities.

- Ensure regular opportunities for curriculum conversations are built into line management meetings.

How will you conduct meaningful curriculum conversations?

- Decide whether curriculum conversations will be had through SLT line managers assigned to different subjects or through one curriculum leader.

- Ensure leaders have the knowledge required to understand the disciplinary uniqueness of the subjects they line manage.

- As leaders, ensure that you engage with the subject discipline of those whom you line manage.

- Train and support leaders to ensure these conversations are effective, particularly if their expertise is either not in curriculum design or not in the subject they line manage.

- Devise a series of questions to be answered during these conversations based on school context, school priorities, subject discipline and stage of curriculum – see Section Four for further insight to how these questions might be framed.

SECTION TWO: SUBJECT LEVEL
SHAPING THE CURRICULUM

Effective whole-school leadership can provide the mechanisms to give subject leaders the time, space and knowledge required for thoughtful and focused curriculum design. The significance of the subject leader's role in shaping the curriculum cannot be understated as it is their expertise that breathes life into the subject. This section offers a framework for exploring the internal dynamics of the curriculum. It helps subject leaders deconstruct and reconstruct their curriculum to ensure it is faithful to the subject discipline and meaningful for their students.

CHAPTER 2
CURRICULUM RATIONALE

As the curriculum lies very much in the hands of each respective subject leader, it is they who we must empower to be the experts. Being able to translate your subject specialism is a craft in itself: as Tom Sherrington proposes, 'Give maximum value to the process, not the products. What matters is that teachers understand their curriculum, the sequence, the choices. This takes time.'[26] Once we free up the time that is necessary for subject leaders to contemplate their curriculum, it is key they feel empowered to do so, but also informed as to what this should look like in practice.

This is more than a straightforward acknowledgement of subject-specific expertise: it requires knowledge and training for subject leaders to do justice to such an important task. In addition, we must ensure that those who teach the curriculum can develop professionally under the expertise of the subject lead. It is this collegiate process that nurtures curricular work at every level. By doing so, we not only work to improve the curriculum menu now, but also nurture curriculum designers of the future. Appositely, the National Foundation for Educational Research (NFER) released a recent report on the tensions between teacher autonomy and satisfaction, and the type of work that feeds these aspects respectively.[27] Handing over a subject to those who adore and are excited by it engages those individuals in work that enriches them professionally.

---

26. https://twitter.com/teacherhead/status/1137007198108889088
27. Worth, J. & Van den Brande, J. (2020) *Teacher autonomy: how does it relate to job satisfaction and retention?* Slough: NFER.

Subject leaders must therefore be empowered to drive their subjects forward. As experts of their discipline, they are best placed to make choices around the substance, form and delivery of their subject. To do this work, we need to avoid poor proxies and quick fixes such as skills tracing or bought-in, contextless curriculum packages that fail to respond to the context of the school or nuances of the subject. Whether as a short-term recovery from burdensome workload, or a remedy for issues of recruitment, such approaches disregard and indeed hinder future development of the subject and of the expertise of the teachers that serve it. With a judicious balance of support and space provided by senior leaders, the subject lead can instead set about the task of designing, critiquing, collaborating and consulting, to enhance their curriculum provision and give students a rich and meaningful experience in their subject.

Developing a culture of collaboration in an environment of continual improvement and review is crucial to this ambition as subject leads not only need to contemplate the issues of their subject, but also nurture those who will enable them to enact it. By establishing the ethos of the subject – its nature and its power – before delving into the minutiae of the discipline itself, subject leaders can immerse themselves in intelligent curriculum thinking to produce something beautiful. Before we can move toward the day-to-day implementation of curriculum, the work of the subject leader is to establish how the knowledge of their subject exists, functions and coexists, before making informed decisions in how to present this to students.

- Subject leaders must be empowered to undertake the work of the curriculum.
- Subject leaders require a deep understanding of the ethos and nature of their subject to make informed decisions for their curriculum.

Powerful knowledge for all

To consider the work ahead for the subject leader, it is worth addressing what schools are for and how our disciplines fulfil this overarching purpose. We must seek to instil a balance of powerful knowledge as a tool for social justice whilst paying heed to how we bring students along in that journey – not just as a school, but as a society. Do we actively work to convey our subject as concrete and meaningful in the context of the wider world?[28]

Students should be exposed to knowledge across a range of academic disciplines that inducts them into a level of 'public understanding'[29] that allows them to think beyond their own experiences to see them reflected in a new way. Where the laws of mathematics seek pattern and order, and art seeks an understanding of beauty and emotion, the powerful knowledge that brings us to these ideas makes visible the patterns and connections that can take students beyond the context of the classroom towards a new way of experiencing the world. As Wheelahan outlines:

> We need to go beyond underlying appearances or events to understand the connections that produce the reality that we experience (Sayer 2000). This is because the world is complex and stratified.[30]

The powerful knowledge required to make these connections is what we offer our students to allow them to consider and reflect on their reality. One of the aims in exposing these patterns is to help students find their own patterns. The function of this powerful knowledge is to support students to become the thinkers of future knowledge: it enables students 'to think the unthinkable and the not yet thought.'[31] Knowledge is generative; the more knowledge the student has, the more the student will learn. An epistemic understanding ensures that students will not only appreciate literature, science, and the arts, but provides the foundation for them to question and critique the world for themselves.

28. Wheelahan, L. M. (2007) 'How competency-based training locks the working class out of powerful knowledge: a modified Bernsteinian analysis', *British Journal of Sociology of Education*, (28), 637–651.

29. Young, M. (2019), keynote speech at the plenary session at the X NIS International Research-to-Practice Conference 'Next Generation Schools', April 2019.

30. Wheelahan, L. M. (2007) 'How competency-based training locks the working class out of powerful knowledge: a modified Bernsteinian analysis', *British Journal of Sociology of Education*, (28), 637–651.

31. Bernstein, B. (2000, 2nd ed.) *Pedagogy, symbolic control and identity: theory, research, critique*. Lanham, MD: Rowman & Littlefield.

Ultimately, it is for us to imbue our students with an understanding of our subjects that goes beyond their school experience in a way that pays service to both the beauty and sophistry of the subject. We should look to reach beyond their immediate context, beyond exam specifications and beyond the remit of a national curriculum framework. If we forget our role as specialists and overlook the capability of our subject to fulfil such a purpose, then we act to deny our students access to enriching and meaningful possibilities, now and in the future. To know the powerful knowledge of your subject is not to dictate its meaning, but to enable students to form a personal connection with this knowledge and in turn, translate it for the world around them. This is why knowledge of our subject is so crucial – if we do not have a deep understanding of our subject, how can we make these choices?

- What is the powerful knowledge of your discipline?
- How does your curriculum seek to move students beyond the 'school experience'?

Diagnosis before treatment

Diagnosis of curriculum requires us to look for common threads, patterns and relationships. Other than the rare case where a subject lead arrives in a school with a curriculum untouched, without ancestry or heritage, there will always need to be an investigation of what has come before, to unravel what must happen next. The work of the curriculum is never done, but a critical audit of the current state of play ensures that we have a clear rationale to carry forward.

To begin this process, we can look to what is least useful and least connected in our curriculum. Which components of the curriculum jar, and do not seem to make sense in relation to the others? Where might the connections be more tenuous between one unit and another, and if that is the case, how do you justify their inclusion? Do key concepts introduced at one particular moment in the curriculum reappear in a more developed form later on?

One example of this might be to collate the key concepts of your discipline and through a deliberate mapping process, outline where students will have the opportunity to visit and revisit these key concepts through a series of rich and developed explorative units within the map as a whole:

Mapping the Connections: 'Substantive Knowledge'

Romans	Anglo-Saxons	Normans	Medieval Realms		Tudors	Stuarts
Conquest	Monarchy	Monarchy	Monarchy	Freedom	Monarchy	Monarchy
Control	Succession	Succession	Religion	Liberty	Succession	Succession
Society	Conquest (invasion)	Conquest	Society		Religion	Parliament
Economy	Control	Militarism (warfare)	Control		Politics	Puritanism
Militarism (warfare)	Hierarchy	Control	Politics		Reform	Civil War
Migration	Society	Society	Civil Rights		Parliament	Warfare
Religion	Economy	Economy	Reform		Puritanism	Republic
	Autocracy	Religion	Autocracy		Warfare	
	Migration	Autocracy	Revolution			

British Empire		Slave Trade	Industrial Revolution	UK Democracy	Civil Rights	
Conquest	Resistance	Economy	Economy	Class	US government	Suffrage
Imperialism	Golden Age	Race relations	Society	Politics	Democracy	Liberty
Nationalism	Colonisation	Resistance (resilience)	Industrialisation	Parliament	Oppression	
Economy	Migration	Control	Class	Society	Segregation	
Control	Liberty	Oppression	Revolution	Suffrage	Integration	
Culture	Militarism	US government	Migration	Liberty	Class	
Genocide	Trade	Civil War	Trade	Control	Reform	
Oppression		Freedom	Laissez faire	Reform	Amendment	
Race Relations		Liberty			Culture	

World War I	Russian Rev'	Inter-War	Roaring 20's	World War II	Holocaust	Cold War / Britain 1945 +
Conquest	Communism	Dictatorship	Golden Age	Conquest	Race Relations	Communism
Militarism	Bolshevism	Fascism	Liberty	Militarism (warfare)	Genocide	Democracy
Alliances	Monarchy	Appeasement	Society	Alliances	Persecution	Society
Imperialism	Socialism	Depression	Culture	Society	Religion	Militarism (warfare)
Nationalism	Autocracy	Political Spectrum	Economy	Colonisation	Oppression	Peace
Dictatorship	Revolution	Collective Security	Laissez Faire	Refuge	Refuge	Migration
Colonisation	Civil War	Peace	Peace	Fascism	Resistance	
	Liberty	Control	Socialism	Control	Culture	
	Republic	Society			Control	

Mapping the connections: substantive knowledge[32]

Subject leads should look to be masters of the process of dissecting and reassembling their curriculum, so that concepts can be articulated as part of the strategic overview of the curriculum as a whole, but also when moving from one unit to the next. To take an example of this in action, students might study the role of gender conformity and rebellion during their curriculum journey within English literature. Introducing students to the representation of gender within Shakespeare's plays could then progress to the way historical female figures rebuked such a representation through their use of language – Pankhurst's speeches were fuelled deliberately with military language to achieve this – which could enable students to further understand the frustrations and limitations of the nameless female within Steinbeck's work, so that when they reach a study of *Macbeth*, they are able to grasp exactly how prominently gender constraint sought to hinder

32. Kindly provided by Colin McCormick of Alsop High School.

the choices of the individual. This simply would not be possible without a thorough, deliberate return to and evolution of the concept over time.

A cohesive curriculum should exist in such a way that it is fairly straightforward to not only identify the relationship of one unit to the next, but also that these connections are deep and meaningful rather than ostensible. This goes beyond simply whether Shakespeare is taught three times and therefore we have a common thread; the patterns and connections across components need to go deeper and be more insightful to help students create meaning and build a stronger schematic framework for the subject. It is the concept and not the content that we seek to revisit. In all disciplines, there are concepts, moments, ideas and language that will either repeat or rhyme. Drawing attention to these and pulling on these threads creates a more meaningful sense of cohesion across the curriculum. A subject lead will be called upon to fulfil this aim, and will need to prepare themselves and their team to undertake the process of disassembly and reassembly, to ensure the curriculum remains continually fit for purpose.

- How have you sought to diagnose your existing curriculum?

The traditions of the discipline

As Aristotle is to philosophy, Archimedes is to mathematics; as Curie is to science, Fontana is to art. There are unequivocal, irremovable foundations of our disciplines that we simply cannot compromise on. If we were looking to provide a gold standard of the subject itself, it would be bordering on sacrilegious to overlook such elements, and without them, our understanding of the subject is skewed.

Science cannot be articulated without an understanding of cells, energy or atomic structure: these are the essential components necessary for further knowledge to be introduced and understood. To study business, we must understand the basic principles of economics. In English, though more contentious, Shakespeare, fairy tales and Romanticism may well be considered in a similar way. The subject cannot exist without such moments – they define and inform it. They are the aspects of the subject that must be known, without compromise, in order to understand the discipline. Their inclusion in the curriculum looks to pay quiet respect to its origins and traditions as part of its ongoing evolution.

- Where do the traditions of your subject feature within your curriculum?

The heritage of the subject

To understand the evolution of our subject and its relationship to the modern world, we need to know its history and the journey it has taken: a sense of heritage that acknowledges changes or developments over time so that we can consider the contentions that our subject has dealt with (or not) and expose students to the subjective and the changeable in our discipline. The theory of gravity should be accompanied by an awareness of the intellectual thinking that came before it; Fermat's last theorem provided a narrative that made the seemingly unsolvable solvable. These moments reveal a hidden corner of the subject itself that is worth exploring if we are to fully induct students into our subject discipline.

This examination of a subject over time should inevitably pull together the contentious issues that remain unresolved for the subject: what do the experts and academics of your field debate over? How has the subject failed to provide definitive answers to the overarching questions of its field? What has yet to be discovered or determined? The debate around the external influences of climate change on the carbon cycle will likely modify how geographers teach both these topics within their classroom; equally, the variances within religions over the last century alone will lead to an evolution of the debate for philosophers and anthropologists alike.

Such points of critique that might remain unanswered will help subject leaders to consider how these moments might be incorporated into the wider strategy for the subject itself. We cannot yet determine how life began, but we can work to determine what we do know about life's origins. We cannot ascertain that there is one true God, but we can work to establish the key beliefs around the Trinity. A consideration of how attempts have been made to respond to such questions helps us to develop critical consumers of our subject who have a relationship with this knowledge, as opposed to being mere conduits of it. This enables students to understand how responsive and fluid our subject disciplines have been and continue to be within the world around them.

- When and how do students learn about the evolution of your subject?

There is no dichotomy

As we shape our curriculum aims, we need to consider what students gain from our subjects – what they will master, what they will experience, how they will begin to make connections and see the world differently. Whilst previously these overarching aims may have resembled a list of skills, this approach does not provide an effective indicator of what students have learned or what they may remember. Of course, some students may develop analytical skills as they progress through a history curriculum, but some do not; are we claiming that these students have gained nothing? ED Hirsch elucidates this:

> Use the word expertise rather than word skills. As soon as you use the word expertise, you recognise there's a knowledge component there, you really have to be an expert about this and that. So core knowledge is trying to figure it out – what are the topics about which it's most important to be an expert.[33]

---

33. Hirsch, E.D. (2015), talk on core knowledge, accessed at https://www.youtube.com/watch?v=XxyFkGYTb5o on 1st June 2020.

Skills do not exist in isolation, they cannot form in a vacuum – substance is required. Skills such as analysis and evaluation are a manifestation of knowledge in practice; they are not our subject discipline, they are the way it manifests. There is no dichotomy here: it is not either/or. Spielman shares that during Ofsted inspections, teachers and school leaders 'did not perceive a tension between knowledge and skill, and instead saw them as intertwined.'[34] Our curriculum therefore needs to acknowledge the relationship between skills and knowledge as coexistent, interdependent and symbiotic.

- Where and how does the curriculum balance knowledge with opportunities to practise what has been learned?

Confidence in articulation

To examine, scrutinise and make choices for our curriculum, we need to be able to articulate its aims, structure, hierarchies and connections both for ourselves and for others. Not for external agencies to measure, or for others to pass judgement or give approval, but as a true demonstration that as subject leader you have taken responsibility for and paid service to the rationale and ethos of your subject. If we are to believe in the work we do and in its power, we need to be clear of its purpose and intentions. Curation of the curriculum means to articulate it without a script or scheme of work, because it reflects the values we have assigned to it. This may be a narration of the rationale behind discarding one unit for another, or a consideration of the sequence chosen for curriculum delivery. It might be that as a subject lead, you are able to explain how your curriculum design honours the heritage of your subject at a local level, and how this contributes to the student's experience of knowledge gained in connection to other key moments within the curriculum as a whole. These values will inform the choices we make in terms of what we include, what we disregard, how it is delivered and how it will evolve. Reinforcing understanding

---

34. Spielman, A. (2018), *Knowledge or skills: what is the real substance of education?* FE News, accessed at https://www.fenews.co.uk/fevoices/19845-knowledge-or-skills-what-is-the-real-substance-of-education.

CHAPTER 3
CURRICULUM KNOWLEDGE

Curriculum design is about choice. It is about choosing what, when, how and to whom we teach. For a long time, the focus of planning and CPD has been predominantly on *how* we teach – often related to generic pedagogical approaches and driven less by a sequenced curriculum and more by a series of activities or different parts of a lesson, such as the need to include a learning objective, starter, main and plenary. We can be too preoccupied with how tasks and activities fit the shape of predetermined lesson structures and lose focus on *what* should be taught and learnt. But it is the 'what' that should hold the power, because it is vital to the subject itself.

As Willingham summarises: 'we remember what we think about'.[35] We need students to be thinking about 'what' we want them to learn. To do so, we need to clearly and explicitly establish what this is and make the 'how' servant to this, thereby empowering teachers to find the best ways to ensure these elements have been learnt: to ensure they have been 'thought' about. This shift ensures learning sequences are designed with this clear aim in mind rather than being focused on activities and tasks which can be a distraction from what we want children to learn. To make informed choices about what is included in our curriculum, we need to understand the interplay between the different types of knowledge that underpin each subject and the extent to which these influence curriculum design.

---

35. Willingham, D. T. (2003) 'How we learn: ask the cognitive scientist. Students remember... what they think about', *American Educator*, 27 (2), 37–41.

To begin, it is worth making distinctions between different types of knowledge and the relationship between them, as this will help to inform not only what we include in the curriculum but also the way it is sequenced. In addition, each type of knowledge comes with a series of questions to ask when deciding what influence it will have on your curriculum and how you will address this.

Core knowledge

This refers to the knowledge we want students to retain in their long-term memory. It forms the cognitive architecture on which they build their understanding, creativity and enquiry. This may include equations, dates and facts, such as the equation for calculating volume or the key plot points and stylistic features of a novel. It may be the physical features of coastlines, or the use of masculine and feminine in the French language. This is the foundational knowledge we want students to recall with automaticity; it provides a foothold for new information and new learning and is what we want students to retain throughout their education.

It is worth noting that what we consider core knowledge is not bound by specifications for national qualifications, though it is likely to feature on them. Not being explicitly referenced on an exam mark scheme does not preclude knowledge from being core. The power of this core knowledge is in the way it can manifest 'indirectly, but powerfully and critically, in future learning of other content',[36] helping unlock future understanding and building stronger schematic architecture.

- How will you map your core knowledge?
- How will you ensure this is secure for all students?
- How will this be returned to over time to ensure it is embedded in long-term memory?

---

36. Counsell, C. (2018) 'Senior curriculum leadership', available at: https://thedignityofthethingblog.wordpress.com/author/christinecounsell/ (accessed 2018).

Hinterland knowledge

Hinterland knowledge refers to the elaborations, embellishments and flourishes that we use to furnish and frame the core knowledge. This may include the narratives, metaphors, analogies or anecdotes we use to reinforce meaning and provide texture to the core knowledge, such as looking at Pre-Raphaelite paintings when teaching *The Lady of Shalott* or *Hamlet,* or embellishing an explanation of vacuum through the tagline from the film *Alien*: 'In space no one can hear you scream'. This hinterland requires the same care, attention and planning that we give to the core knowledge because although its function within the curriculum is enriching and vital, it can also fall foul of becoming a distraction.

As Christine Counsell explains:

> Of course, the distinction doesn't work in all subjects all the time. For in some subjects, reduction to the pure propositions is vital and the last thing one wants is contextual stuff. Even context can be clutter. But that is the very reason why we need the word 'hinterland'. It helps us distinguish between a vital property that makes curriculum work as narrative and merely 'engaging activities' which can distract and make pupils think about (and therefore remember) all the wrong things.[37]

Therefore, our hinterland requires careful thought and balance: we must consider what core knowledge we need students to have remembered, ensuring our hinterland pays service to this and does not act to conceal or distract from what we want students to remember. If, when we ask students to later recall what they were taught in a previous lesson and the hinterland is all that remains, we have either not struck that balance or we have misunderstood what constitutes effective hinterland. To illustrate this further:

---

37. Counsell, C. (2018) 'The indirect manifestation of knowledge: a curriculum as a narrative', available at: https://thedignityofthethingblog.wordpress.com/2018/04/07/senior-curriculum-leadership-1-the-indirect-manifestation-of-knowledge-a-curriculum-as-narrative/ (accessed 28th May 2020).

A maths teacher, with a fragile understanding of what is considered hinterland knowledge, decides to use Wimbledon to teach mean, median and mode. The teacher scours the internet for ticket tariffs and asks students to decide how much the public should be charged depending on whether they watch Serena Williams or Andy Murray. The discussion then becomes a debate of which tennis player is worthy of a higher ticket price and whether different seats should have different tariffs. In two weeks, when the teacher returns to calculations for mean, median or mode, the class recalls very little, except they now know the names of two tennis players.

We can return to Willingham: 'we remember what we think about'.[38] What students have thought about here are tennis players and match tickets and this is what they have remembered. This is not hinterland; it does not embody, enrich or pay service to the core knowledge and instead it becomes a distraction.

There are various ways we can ensure that our curriculum planning uses hinterland knowledge in a way that is meaningful and purposeful but above all aids the student to learn in such a way that knowledge is retained. If with some questioning and teasing out, students can use this hinterland and follow its threads back to the core, then its function is maintained. However, if this hinterland knowledge becomes either a distraction or is so far removed from the core knowledge that it loses its utility, then we need to address this.

We can look to achieve a sense of balance through an understanding of curiosity and how its function can influence our planning of knowledge throughout the curriculum. Ian Leslie proposes that 'curiosity does not exist in a vacuum';[39] instead we seek to open up information gaps, close them, and open them up again. Curiosity is therefore dependent upon our existing knowledge and on the interplay between core and hinterland.

---

38. Willingham, D. T. (2003) 'How we learn: ask the cognitive scientist. Students remember... what they think about', *American Educator*, 27 (2), 37–41.

39. Leslie, I. (2014) *Curious: The Desire to Know and Why Your Future Depends on It.* Hachette.

Take an explanation of the solar system. Being taught that Saturn is not the only ringed planet is mildly interesting and this addresses some factual core knowledge about Saturn. However, even if this detail contradicts common knowledge, it is fairly prosaic and barely piques our curiosity: it is dissatisfying, momentary and does not go much beyond a simplistic feature-spotting exercise. Now consider adding to this explanation that Jupiter is also ringed but these rings differ to those of Saturn because not only are they less visible to the naked eye but they are composed of dust not ice, and so were only discovered some 40 years ago. Then we can elaborate that the dust that formed these rings was not incidental, but is the detritus left by meteors striking the surface of Jupiter's inner moons.

In a religious education lesson, hinterland may be used to reinforce students' understanding of incarnation. To define incarnation as encompassing both the form of man and God is simply two-dimensional, but also problematic when applied to later readings of the New Testament. It would undoubtedly force the teacher to reteach incarnation as a construct when they later teach the crucifixion and resurrection of Christ. If the teacher chose to initially teach incarnation through the hinterland knowledge of the book of Luke, sharing the symbolism of the gifts offered by the Magi, the depiction of the humble stable in contrast to the praise and worship bestowed upon the child makes this understanding of incarnation both deeper and more concrete.

These rich details work to tantalise our curiosity and they function to amplify the core knowledge without becoming a distraction. It follows then that curiosity is not necessarily aroused by core knowledge, but by its surrounding narrative; we tussle between 'diversive curiosity' where we seek out fleeting information for the sake of its novelty and excitement, and a steady reliance upon 'epistemic curiosity' which is more thoughtful, sustained and requires discipline and focus.[40]

---

40. Leslie explores this interplay in detail in *Curious: The Desire to Know and Why Your Future Depends on It* (Hachette, 2014).

The interplay of the diverse and epistemic acts to ultimately maintain attention and, in turn, evoke a desire for knowledge. Our hinterland can therefore act as a gateway for students' desire to learn and understand more; what is seemingly ephemeral knowledge that piques students' diverse curiosity is the very knowledge that can encourage epistemic curiosity, creating momentum for sustained learning and investigation, leading to new insights and deeper learning. For example, details of the life of Mary Shelley may offer a moment of diversive curiosity but could in turn provoke epistemic curiosity, resulting in a more detailed study and interest in her work and that of the Romantics. By mapping the interaction between the core and hinterland, we seek to achieve this process of teasing out, then pulling back, so that students make their own connections between the two and begin to delight in their pursuit.

- How have you decided on the hinterland knowledge for your subject?
- How will you ensure that this is balanced so it does not become a distraction?
- How will collaborative planning inform this hinterland knowledge?

Substantive knowledge

Substantive knowledge refers to the body of facts, principles, laws, descriptions, concepts, claims or accounts of a subject, and will likely form the basis for much of the core knowledge we teach. The unities of time, space and action according to Aristotle's Poetics, the rules of netball, atomic structures, and the events leading up to World War I are all examples of substantive knowledge. Much of our substantive knowledge will be driven by the national curriculum or by examination specifications, but we can look to enhance and exceed this with the choices we make.

Choices regarding substantive knowledge are also likely to be more difficult in some subjects than in others. Science and maths teachers can only look on in bemusement whilst English teachers appear to have an existential crisis about the substantive knowledge to teach. Whilst for some subjects the choices are perhaps more limited, English and many other humanities have a vast body to choose from and have far less explicit direction imposed on them. However, with our finite curriculum, it is worth choosing our substantive knowledge through a consideration of its flexibility, versatility and, of course, its beauty. In English, this is often related to text choice; in history this might be a decision of timeframe or location; in religious education this may be a question of theological or philosophical perspective.

In whichever case, choices need to be made based on how much this substantive knowledge lends itself to enhancing wider schema. For example, texts chosen in English need to work very hard as they will need to encompass a range of concepts, ideas, contexts and features in order to offer the elasticity required for them to be worth the limited curriculum time that can be given over to them. However, we should not lose sight of the value that such texts have. This value is inextricably linked to their beauty and their richness – it is their ability to bring understanding but also joy to the curriculum. Literary texts, religious parables and historical stories, 'are not merely handmaidens for illustrating a concept. Narratives matter in their own right.'[41] Therefore, our choices should encompass both usefulness and beauty.

Finally, the substantive knowledge we choose will often act as a bridge or precursor for what may come later, acting as a threshold and helping to connect the intertextual webs required for deeper understanding. Therefore, the choice of substantive knowledge at one juncture of the curriculum may influence what needs to be included before or after.

- What is the substantive knowledge of your subject? This is likely to form a significant part of your curriculum design.
- How will you choose which substantive knowledge will be included in your curriculum?
- How will you ensure that it is both functional and beautiful?

---

41. Counsell, C. (2020), 'Better Conversations with Subject Leaders' in C. Sealy & T. Bennet (eds.), *The researchED Guide to the Curriculum*. John Catt.

Disciplinary knowledge

Disciplinary knowledge addresses the way a particular field generates and verifies knowledge. Again, Counsell offers an authoritative and eloquent depiction, describing this as:

> ...that part of the subject where pupils understand each discipline as a tradition of inquiry with its own distinctive pursuit of truth. For each subject is just that: a product and an account of an ongoing truth quest, whether through empirical testing in science, argumentation in philosophy/history, logic in mathematics or beauty in the arts.[42]

The extent to which disciplinary knowledge features in our curriculum is subject dependent and there is no measurement of how much disciplinary knowledge should be included and nor should we ever try to have one: we are not aiming for a tick-box curriculum which includes all the different knowledge types as a measure of a gold standard. The mathematics curriculum in secondary education involves little if any disciplinary knowledge because it requires knowledge of mathematical models, interpretation and questioning at a level so flexible and so secure for students to meaningfully partake in the disciplinary discovery and investigation of mathematics, that this is likely beyond the capacity of this stage of their educational or curriculum journey. That is not to say that students should not be exposed to what mathematicians do and how they come to make claims of mathematical modelling – they absolutely should. However, a focus on disciplinary knowledge in mathematics which asks students to attempt to design their own models is unlikely to be effective as they simply do not have the epistemic or schematic framework for this to be a fruitful pursuit.

On the other hand, subjects such as history concern themselves a great deal with disciplinary knowledge: this is often placed at the centre of the

---

42. Counsell, C. (2018) 'Taking the Curriculum Seriously', *Impact: Journal of the Chartered College of Teaching*.

history curriculum as it deals with the significance of judgement, causation, conclusions and bias, all of which are at the heart of the discipline. Whereas, religious education as a subject draws upon a number of disciplines, such as philosophy, anthropology, ethics, social sciences, history and art. Contentions therefore arise as to which of these disciplines serve to provide a focus for the religious education curriculum and which may be more periphery. An understanding of the accompanying disciplines that shape subjects such as religious education can help to inform the rationale for the curriculum and provide its framework, whether approached through the lens of theology or philosophy, ethics or social sciences, or all of these combined. In English, how we come to conclusions about the value of texts and what has influenced their style and form – such as the way one literary movement or theory builds on what has preceded it – also forms a significant part of the discipline; the evolution of the subject informs how it should be taught.

Students need to understand that texts, sources, ideas and debates do not happen in a vacuum and that social, cultural and political shifts are mirrored by the work of that time. Through this, we can bring students into the discussion of who decides what is canon, or the subjectivity of historical 'truth', or the history of mathematical discovery that predates and travels far further than Western civilisation. Doing so allows us to debate and discuss how we come to conclusions within a culture, as well as offering insight into the inextricable link between the subject discipline and the power structures and systems that have helped direct and embed it. These debates offer a richness and understanding of the subject that may otherwise be overlooked.

Sequencing disciplinary knowledge

When we teach the disciplinary aspects of our subject, we need to make decisions about whether these form a discrete unit of work – which is then referred back to during subsequent teaching – or whether this is threaded through all of our curriculum with the explicit teaching of disciplinary factors each time they arise. In English, there could be a discrete unit on the history of literary movements, which is returned to when texts connected to these movements are taught later. Whilst history, by its nature, is more likely to tightly weave the disciplinary and the substantive throughout. The science curriculum, on the other hand, may begin with an initial precis of the scientific method which is then returned to each time students collect and evaluate scientific evidence. Understanding the role of disciplinary knowledge within a subject helps us make choices around what to include in our curriculum and where, and will affect how the substantive knowledge is presented and treated.

Disciplinary knowledge and recontextualisation

In our exploration of disciplinary knowledge, it is worth noting Bernstein's contention that curriculum is an act of recontextualisation: that the curriculum 'selectively appropriates, relocates, refocuses, and relates [the subject discipline] to constitute its own order.'[43] This results in practice in the classroom being different to that in the discipline itself: our students' first experience of our subject may not be entirely representative of the subject within the wider world. When considering the way disciplinary knowledge informs our curriculum planning, we need to not only be sensitive to the nuances between and within subjects but also to those created by their recontextualisation. We need to find ways for students to be inducted into both the discipline within the field and in the wider world, and to understand its reconfiguration for the classroom.

As Ruth Ashbee proposes: 'we must ask what it means to practise the subject in the mostly scholarly way – [remaining] faithful to the subject discipline.'[44] Literature academics do not study texts through the same lens as the questions on a GCSE exam, nor do they write using formulaic paragraph structures; the scholarly pursuit of English bears little resemblance to what sometimes constitutes English in the classroom.

---

43. Bernstein, B. (2000) *Pedagogy, Symbolic Control, and Identity*. Lanham, MD: Rowman and Littlefield.
44. In her contributing chapter, Ashbee further analyses and applies Bernstein's work, offering an elegant treatise in disciplinary examination.

Instead then, students should become more practised in the analysis and critique of literature that is closer to that of academics, as soon as the knowledge required to do so is secured.

To develop this notion of remaining faithful to the subject discipline further, it is one of the reasons that the geography qualification at GCSE demands fieldwork as part of the programme of study, or why drama requires students to be assessed for taking on roles that exist within the technical department of a theatre, such as being responsible for set design or assuming the role of puppeteer. These subjects, although recontextualised for the classroom, retain some of the key disciplinary elements of their field of production. Whereas in science, the gap between the classroom and the field of production is somewhat wider. In science lessons, experiments aim to prove what is already known to be true, whereas the discipline in the field tests theories with the aim to disprove what is 'known' to either strengthen or discount current thinking. By drawing attention to this, we can attempt to narrow the gap between the discipline in the field and the discipline experienced in the classroom. This provides students with a better understanding of our subject whilst also being conscious of this recontextualisation, as we navigate and attempt to ward against the disfiguration of our subject through policy and misapplied pedagogy.

- Where are there opportunities to investigate the disciplinary aspect of your subject?
- When are students exposed to the arguments and debates involved in coming to a sense of 'truth' in your subject or the foundations on which your subject is built?
- Will aspects of the discipline be taught explicitly and discretely?
- How will the choices around substantive knowledge best support students' understanding of these aspects of the discipline?
- How will you ensure that the subject is practised in a way that is faithful to the subject discipline?

Declarative knowledge

Declarative knowledge is sometimes referred to as propositional knowledge or the 'know-that' of a subject. For example, you can know that the angles in a triangle equal 180 degrees, that cuneiform was one of the earliest forms of writing, and that Charles Dickens wrote *Oliver Twist*. There is clearly some cross-over here between declarative and substantive knowledge: what is important is the understanding that although declarative knowledge does not necessarily translate to application, application is impossible without declarative knowledge.

This understanding of declarative knowledge can ensure we move away from decontextualised skills. We may want our students to enquire, create, synthesise and evaluate, but this requires declarative knowledge to do so. Daisy Christodoulou adroitly illustrates this point when discussing Shakespeare.[45] Shakespeare's source material for *Othello* is based on his knowledge of Cinthio's *Hecatommithi*, just as his description of Cleopatra's procession along the river Cydnus echoes North's translations of *Plutarch*. Shakespeare's knowledge of history, rhetoric, religion and mythology is what underpins his creativity – it is this knowledge that shapes his writing. We cannot know how to do something in a vacuum – we need declarative knowledge first.

- What declarative knowledge will you include in your curriculum?
- How will you ensure your curriculum does not ask students to apply, create, synthesise or evaluate in a vacuum?

Procedural knowledge

Sometimes referred to as skill or technique, procedural knowledge refers to the 'know-how' of the processes required in a subject. This might include solving simultaneous equations, constructing a thesis statement, drawing a graph, or the actions required to perform a somersault. To make decisions related to map-reading in geography, students would need to first be taught the procedure for following grid references – whilst a

---

45.   Christodoulou, C. (2016), 'Shakespeare and Creative Education', *The Use of English*, 67 (2).

student learning French would benefit from being taught a process for deconstructing and then reconstructing sentences in order to translate texts from French to English. Knowing these procedures does not necessarily mean you can do them well. However, explicitly teaching the procedural knowledge for a task removes some of the guesswork, allowing students to focus on the task itself and to practise the processes required, rather than becoming frustrated by not only struggling with the task but also having to work out how to approach it in the first place.

Collaborative planning and common language around teaching procedural knowledge is crucial. Firstly, the combined expertise of the department will help come to decisions about the methods and processes being taught, helping to ensure that the most effective of these will be chosen. Secondly, as students move through the school, retaining similar methods and procedures will help them to master the process rather than expending time, energy and working memory attempting new methods according to the teacher that takes their class.

By establishing commonality, we build a sense of cohesion into our approach. Is it more precise to use the term connective or conjunction? Is it truer to the subject to refer to germs or pathogens? How do we know which is most effective, or more faithful? We can also use the knowledge of the procedures previously taught to decide where, why and how we may vary an approach and make more informed decisions in doing so. Knowing that a class has previously been taught one method allows us to consider when and how variations may be used to strengthen students' expertise later. This consistency of approach not only helps to activate and reinforce prior learning and bring more precision to our explanations, it can also help reduce workload as resources can be framed by these methods, making it simpler to return to them each time the process is referred to in a new context.

Live modelling of these processes and procedures, and a granular approach to breaking down the steps required, needs to be built into the curriculum with plenty of time and opportunity to explicitly teach and practise these procedures using a common language and consistent methodology. Once these procedures are mastered, students will be able to complete tasks with automaticity and begin to experiment in other contexts independently. Take for example the procedural knowledge required to calculate the perimeter of simple shapes. If this process is repeated and taught in the same way until the steps are mastered with automaticity, the procedural knowledge becomes more flexible and can then be applied to contexts such as calculating the missing side of a polygon. Equally, using Hochmann's 'because, but, so' methodology to expand explanations[46] enables students to use this as a framework for articulating their ideas. Using procedural knowledge in repeated practice of the subject or subjects allows students to focus their attention on the content of the subject itself.

- What is the procedural knowledge of your subject?
- How will the steps of these procedures be broken down and modelled?
- Where is common language and methodology required to reinforce students' competence and understanding?
- How often will students practise these procedures?

---

46. Hochman, J. & Wexler, N. (2017) *The Writing Revolution.* Jossey-Bass.

CHAPTER 4
CURRICULUM SEQUENCING

Once we begin to better understand the interplay of knowledge in our subject, we can use this to inform how we sequence the curriculum. If a curriculum is to be coherent and follow a logical progression, attention needs to be paid to the order in which knowledge, in whatever form that might take, should be introduced and returned to. The curriculum in many subjects is dependent on a deliberate approach to the sequencing of knowledge because one concept often relies on the understanding of what has come previously and what will come next. Effective sequencing can also provide a way of embellishing and unifying what may otherwise seem like disconnected fragments of knowledge. To create a sense of coherence for the discipline that we teach, we need to ask ourselves: *Why this? Why now?*

Cognitive load theory

Cognitive load theory informs our curriculum sequencing by revealing the role of memory in helping students build the cognitive architecture required to access the curriculum effectively. As working memory is limited, we need to sequence our curriculum to reduce cognitive load by drawing on prior knowledge and logically sequencing episodes of learning so they accumulate in small stages, securing understanding at one stage before moving on to the next. This assists in reducing cognitive load as students can draw more effectively from their long-term memory, thereby reducing the load for their working memory.[47]

---

47 Sweller, J. (1994). Cognitive load theory, learning difficulty, and instructional design. *Learn. Instr.* 4: 295–312.

Although activating prior knowledge is an effective method for reducing cognitive load, this needs always to serve new learning. Take for example a history teacher introducing the concept of colonialism through a study of the British Empire. Students need to access a working definition of 'empire', relying on their understanding of vocabulary such as 'monarchy' and 'reign'. The teacher then provides an explanation of imperialism, with a brief allusion to their previous teaching of Russia the year before, polished off with the image of Queen Victoria's statue that displays the words 'The entitlement of Great Britain' underneath. In this example, prior knowledge functions as extraneous load: students are left grappling with their working definitions of key terms and their recognition of Queen Victoria, alongside a plethora of completely new information, made more complicated by attempting to draw from their prior knowledge, as prompted by the teacher, with very little context. If, however, the teacher opened the lesson with a retrieval task that prompted students to recall the definitions of 'empire', 'monarchy' and 'reign' and framed these within the context of the lesson – making explicit the connection between Queen Victoria and the British Empire's role in widespread colonisation – then cognitive load is well-managed and the activation of prior knowledge is purposeful for the lesson, resulting in the delivery being far more cohesive and ensuring one idea connects to and informs the next.

Whilst careful sequencing can support new learning by exposing its relationship to prior knowledge, we need to ensure its activation does not contribute to extraneous load. When sequencing learning we need to judiciously select the knowledge most likely to support and connect to new learning so that we do not unintentionally hinder students' understanding. This requires a systematic, streamlined approach to the activation of prior knowledge with explicit connections between what has been learnt and what is to come next so that these connections strengthen students' cognitive architecture rather than act as an extraneous distraction.

- An understanding of cognitive load theory can inform our curriculum sequencing.

- Logical sequencing of the curriculum supports the activation of prior knowledge, which can reduce cognitive load.
- Activation of prior knowledge should be carefully planned to ensure this does not unintentionally contribute to extraneous load.
- Making explicit connections between pre-existing knowledge and new knowledge strengthens students' cognitive architecture.

Coherence and connections

Sequencing of the curriculum is clearly more than the ordering of its component parts – it is about the relationships and connections between them, and the deeper understanding that the sequence allows our students to access. It is more than simply: this, follows this, follows this – it is narrative, it tells the story of our subject, it is a conversation between its parts.

However, curriculum design can sometimes be reduced to 'fragments of knowledge [that] float around without being placed in a coherent structure',[48] or in some cases, disjointed units of work merely connected by the command words of GCSE exam papers with no real sense of cohesion. We begin to move towards a better model when we start to see how one episode of teaching requires prior knowledge to not only reinforce memory but to access new learning.

However, teaching one unit and then returning to some of the core knowledge of that unit later as a bolt-on exercise in retrieval practice is unlikely to have the desired effect of creating strong schematic models for students. The approach we take in activating prior knowledge needs to pay service to the internal dynamics of our subjects, which are complex, transformational and symbiotic. When returning to key knowledge, we must undertake a revisiting that digs deeper than simple retrieval: we need to explicitly draw attention to where we have seen this vocabulary, concept, behaviour or pattern before and expose its relationship to what

---

48. Myatt. M, (2018) 'Building Curriculum', *Impact: Journal of the Chartered College of Teaching*, https:// impact.chartered.college/article/building-curriculum-coherence/.

we are teaching now. It is a process that involves foreshadowing, reference, embellishment, echoes and evolution – a continuous ebbing and flowing between the simple and the esoteric rather than a mere layering of one building block on top of the other. This could be as simple as using signposting statements: *Where have we seen this before? What does this remind us of? How does this have a relationship with what happened previously? How does our understanding of the previous concept inform our understanding of this one?* To sequence our curriculum in a way that is sensitive to and prioritises these internal dynamics, we need to have some understanding of how this works in our subject and how we can harness this when designing our curriculum.

- How do we move beyond simple retrieval and towards strong schematic connections?
- How will the sequence of your curriculum reinforce the relationship between its component parts?

Knowledge structures

To understand the relationship between the components of our curriculum, we need to consider how structures of knowledge affect their sequencing. For the purposes of curriculum sequencing, we can broadly divide knowledge structures into those which are hierarchical and those which are cumulative. However, this is more a question of comparatives than superlatives. Subjects may be more hierarchical than others or more cumulative, but to simply define them as distinctly one or the other would be to oversimplify the nuances of these definitions and the subjects they apply to.

Broadly, subjects such as English literature, religious education, geography, history, art, drama and music may be considered more cumulative than hierarchical as there are fewer threshold concepts[49] that require one component being taught before the next. Although units of study may be related, they are less likely to be reliant on each other for understanding – the curriculum is not forced into a predetermined sequence. However,

---

49. See 'Threshold Concepts' page 67.

subjects with more cumulative structures still benefit from unifying principles to reinforce an understanding of the subject discipline.

Both English literature and history may benefit from chronological sequences of knowledge and include some threshold concepts that offer a gateway to deeper and transformative understanding, such as the role of genre and narrative in English or the effect of bias and subjectivity in history. These modify students' understanding of the subject and so bear significance in curriculum sequencing. In English, these chronological sequences, whether within one unit or across the curriculum as a whole, help students to understand the subject as a discipline, both in terms of how the texts came into being and in terms of their place within history and culture. This also helps students to recognise literature as a force for social change and political commentary, offering a better understanding of the power of great literature. Therefore, although the knowledge structures may be cumulative, there are underlying principles that can be used to give shape and form to the curriculum and assist students in gaining a deeper understanding of the subject.

Subjects such as maths, science and languages, including English language in the teaching of grammar, tend to have more hierarchical structures of knowledge. These are more sensibly arranged within a predetermined order or hierarchy as later knowledge tends to be dependent on students' understanding of prior knowledge. A curriculum for teaching foreign languages, for example, requires a somewhat hierarchical structure; the linguistic structures prevalent within many European languages require students to begin to learn the language through phonology and morphology, before we can even attempt to dissect syntax or semantics. It is why the acquisition of language is rarely effective if we simply learn nouns and verbs without context: to grasp *les hommes sont allés trouver le chat dans les bois*, we must understand the use of *allés* alongside *trouver*. To translate in isolation is insufficient: 'everything find' is nonsensical, but once we understand the relationship between the role of the verb *allés* as both past tense and conditional, we can then start to build a more complete understanding of the statement in its entirety. Knowledge of the noun is not enough, but it is our starting block to then comprehend the relationship between one word and the next.

In subjects where structures of knowledge are more hierarchical, certain prior knowledge is a prerequisite for later understanding, and sequencing decisions are therefore likely to be more passenger than driver.

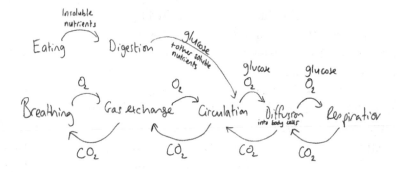

A model of finer sequencing for a lesson on the respiratory system, which displays how the hierarchical structures of knowledge informs its order[50]

This understanding of knowledge structures and unifying principles is not only important for the overarching sequence of the curriculum, but also for shorter episodes of learning, such as the planning of a single lesson or even single explanation. As illustrated in the model above, an understanding of hierarchies allows us to break down knowledge into its smallest constituent parts and begin to work out which order they best fit. The more we break these down and better understand their relationship or levels of reliance, the more finely tuned our planning becomes.

- How do the structures of knowledge in your subject inform its sequencing?

---

50. https://mcsbrent.co.uk/bunsen-blue-designing-a-science-curriculum/, accessed May 2020.

- How can these structures of knowledge inform both the macro and micro considerations required for planning and curriculum design?

Threshold concepts

When considering the structures of knowledge in our curriculum and the hierarchies and unifiers that help students to understand our subject, we can look to the threshold concepts that underpin our subjects and the transformational function these concepts can serve. For more hierarchical subjects, these threshold concepts can offer the foundation for curriculum sequencing. Threshold concepts are not just 'big ideas' or 'key concepts'; they are much more than this. In physics, centre of gravity is a key concept, but it is not a threshold concept. The concept of gravity itself *is* a threshold concept as it transforms our understanding. A threshold concept acts to help students not only access the next stage of learning but can also reconfigure their prior learning. Threshold concepts are described by Myer and Land as 'akin to a portal opening up new and previously inaccessible ways of thinking about something. It represents a transformed way of understanding, or interpreting, or viewing something without which the learner cannot progress.'[51]

Threshold concepts therefore act as a gateway to more knowledge and understanding and help to form stronger schematic frameworks. However, their role in curriculum sequencing and in our understanding of schema and cognition goes further than simply deciding where in the curriculum they may be introduced. They have been described as the 'jewels of the curriculum' as they help teachers to identify areas that require mastery before moving to the next stage of learning, as well as helping to identify where students may struggle to grasp later concepts or where there may be a 'bottleneck' occurring that is preventing students from moving their understanding to the next stage. Identifying and addressing where these threshold concepts are to be taught, retaught, reviewed and refined will help address misconceptions and create stronger schematic architecture. As Land et al explain:

---

51. Meyer, J. H. F. & Land, R. (2005) 'Threshold concepts and troublesome knowledge (2): epistemological considerations and a conceptual framework for teaching and learning', *Higher Education*, 49, 373–388.

A focus on these jewels allows for richer and more complex insights into aspects of the subjects students are studying; it plays a diagnostic role in alerting tutors to areas of the curriculum where students are likely to encounter troublesome knowledge and experience conceptual difficulty.[52]

According to Meyer and Land, threshold concepts have a number of common characteristics that need to be taken into account in our curriculum planning.

Transformative

Firstly, threshold concepts are *transformative* and result in a significant shift in students' thinking. In English, once exposed to the threshold concept of narrative structure, plays, stories, novels or even TV shows and films may take on new meaning, and not only for those experienced *after* having learnt about this concept; it can also reshape previous experiences or understanding. Therefore, threshold concepts are clearly crucial to our students' deeper understanding of the subject, transforming not only what will be taught but also what has previously been taught.

- Which threshold concepts are transformative and can be used to unlock students' understanding of your subject?

Irreversible

Threshold concepts are also *irreversible* – once learned they are unlikely to be unlearned. However, they may still be modified or rejected if they are met with refined or rival conceptual understanding. The concept of photosynthesis, for example, is often modified throughout a students' primary and secondary education, but at each stage it is required to open a different gateway of understanding, whether that is related to respiration, reproduction, food chains or combustion.

---

52. Meyer, J. H. F., Land, R. & Davies, P. (2006) 'Implications of threshold concepts for course design and evaluation', in J. H. F. Meyer & R. Land (eds.), *Overcoming Barriers to Student Understanding: threshold concepts and troublesome knowledge.* London: Routledge.

- How can we acknowledge the irreversibility of a threshold concept whilst being mindful that it may need to be modified or rejected later?

Integrative

The example of photosynthesis also displays the *integrative* nature of threshold concepts as it exposes the interrelatedness of ideas and concepts, helping students make connections that were previously hidden. Explicitly drawing students' attention to these concepts reveals the wider connections and interrelatedness of seemingly episodic or isolated knowledge and helps to form a schematic framework that reinforces understanding not just of the concept itself, but also of all the other concepts and ideas it relates to.

- How can we use threshold concepts to draw students' attention to the connections and patterns of our subjects?

Bounded

Threshold concepts are also often *bounded* or limited to the contexts they are expressed within, and therefore often serve a very specific and limited purpose. As such, they are likely to be tightly woven into the discipline of one subject and are unlikely to transfer to another – in fact doing so can result in misconceptions across disciplines. This notion is perhaps best illustrated by the meaning attributed to specialist terminology in one subject that contradicts its use either in other subjects or in everyday conversation. The term 'contract', for example, has very different meanings in its scientific definition, legal definition and its everyday definition. The use and grammatical rules for verbs in English take a very different form in French. Caution must then be paid to how this 'boundedness' affects curriculum planning both within and across subjects.

- How can we draw students' attention to the boundedness of threshold concepts to address misconceptions across disciplines?

Troublesome

Threshold concepts can be *troublesome* as their complexity can sometimes exceed the level of the learner, yet they need to be introduced to help students access and understand the next stage of their learning. We are therefore left with needing to teach a complex concept that students may not be ready for but which needs to be taught in order to access what is to come next. Nevertheless, this is not to say we should avoid teaching these concepts based on their complexity, particularly given their transformative power. Our awareness of this simply means we need to take special care in our explanation and modelling of these concepts and pay attention to this when collaboratively planning in our department. Having an agreed explanation or common language for these concepts ensures that not only are we drawing on the knowledge and expertise of our department, which is likely to provide students with the best chance of understanding the concept, but will also help students to recognise these concepts when they bump against them later, both in their short- and long-term progression through the curriculum.

The troublesome nature of these concepts lies not only in this form of complexity but also in that they can appear to be 'counterintuitive, alien (emanating from another culture or discourse), or seemingly incoherent',[53] and therefore understanding of a concept may be hindered by the notion that it goes against common sense or intuition. The nature of some concepts may require a reversal of intuitive thought, which can be uncomfortable and challenging for students. In maths, this could be the concept of infinity or imaginary numbers, in English this may be Barthes' concept of the 'death of the author', and in art this might involve ideas around authorship, appropriation and ideological processes.

- How can we address the troublesome complexity of the threshold concepts students need for them to access the next stage of their learning, whilst not undermining or oversimplifying the concept?

---

53. Meyer, J. H. F. & Land, R. (2003) 'Threshold concepts and troublesome knowledge (1): linkages to ways of thinking and practising', in C. Rust (ed.), *Improving Student Learning – ten years on*. Oxford: OCSLD.

Discursive and re-constitutive

In further writing, Meyer et al articulate two additional characteristics of threshold concepts: they are *discursive* and *re-constitutive*.[54] The discursive nature of threshold concepts means that acquiring the concept enhances and extends students' use and understanding of disciplinary language. Understanding of these concepts moves students from a mimicry of language to its meaningful use. Threshold concepts of evolution, ecology, metabolism, genetics and variation all open up a greater understanding of the discourse of biology. Similarly, complex numbers open up discourses surrounding abstraction, imaginary numbers and real numbers in maths. Teaching these concepts results in a discursive shift as the language of these concepts slots together to move students from mimicry of key terms to a deeper understanding of them.

Threshold concepts are also re-constitutive. This characteristic addresses the 'liminal state' in which students move towards an understanding of a concept before its complete grasp, which 'requires a reconfiguring of the learner's prior conceptual schema and letting go or distancing of any earlier conceptual stance'.[55] This liminality describes the oscillation between states of understanding, uncertainty and even regression. This oscillation reinforces the need for concepts to be taught, retaught, reviewed and revised. Each time we refer to or return to these concepts, we must ensure that prior knowledge has been securely retained and students have moved away from any uncertainty, regression or naivety in their understanding.

- Which threshold concepts induct students into the language of our subjects to enhance their understanding?
- How can we address the liminality of these threshold concepts through their re-teaching, revision and review?

54. J. H. F. Meyer & R. Land (eds.), *Overcoming Barriers to Student Understanding: threshold concepts and troublesome knowledge*. London: Routledge.
55. Meyer, J. H. F. & Land, R. (2010) *Threshold Concepts and Transformational Learning*. Boston: Sense Publishers.

The power of threshold concepts

Our curriculums can often become crowded by all that we want to expose students to in our subject and it can be difficult to decide what to discard and what remains. Identifying and understanding the nature of threshold concepts in our subject allows us to make informed decisions about what to include and when, and doing so becomes transformative in itself. This process can also help us to identify where misconceptions are likely to arise and, by returning to the threshold concepts, how these may be addressed.

However, Meyer et al warn against attempting to make threshold concepts easier for students by simplifying their initial introduction, as this can lead to a naive understanding and a result in mimicry of that naive conception rather than deep understanding.[56] Taking time with departments and subject communities to plan such explanations is therefore crucial to ward against these naive conceptions.

Finally, threshold concepts draw our attention to the iterative nature of knowledge acquisition, as these concepts often require regular reinforcement, review and revision to help students access the next stage in their learning. The troublesome and often complex nature of threshold concepts means that it is likely to require several attempts at teaching and explaining before the necessary integration and connection takes place for them to have their transformative effect. Therefore, our understanding of this characteristic can inform our curriculum sequencing both in terms of linear progression through different concepts and in terms of the iterative sequencing necessary to ensure these are regularly returned to.

- What are the threshold concepts of your curriculum?
- How will these be returned to and reinforced?
- How will you close the knowledge gaps for students who have not grasped these concepts?
- How can your understanding of the threshold concepts in your curriculum help to identify and address 'bottlenecks' in learning?

---

56. Ibid.

Meaningful interdisciplinarity

To strengthen students' understanding in one subject, we can look to the interplay of knowledge between related subjects. As Claire Sealy articulates, 'each time a concept is encountered within a different context, not only is the concept more likely to be remembered, the understanding of that concept becomes more nuanced.'[57] However, this is at times interpreted as promoting topic or project based learning or can result in forced surface connections, rather than meaningful interdisciplinarity.

Take the example of war poetry in English being taught at the same time as World War I in history. This could be beneficial, if our English and history departments collaborate on the explicit connections they will be making across their respective subjects and ensure that these are accurate and meaningful. However, if our English teacher brings their own fragile knowledge or even misconceptions of history into the English classroom, this has consequences for teaching in both subjects. History teachers may despair at the claim in English that teaching *The Boy in the Striped Pyjamas* offers an interdisciplinary connection to history, as the text reinforces many misconceptions around World War II, the Holocaust, concentration camps and the school system in Nazi Germany,[58] which then needs to be unlearnt in history lessons. Instead, if we engage with how the knowledge in one subject can reinforce understanding in another and use this to collaboratively plan meaningful interdisciplinary explanations, we can avoid reinforcing misconceptions or paying lip service to cross-curricular connections.

Collaboratively mapping the vocabulary that reinforces interdisciplinary understanding across history and English is also likely to be a fruitful exercise in creating more cross-curricular cohesion. Where concepts are not 'bounded', the explicit teaching and reference to terms such as 'monarchy', 'society', 'poverty' or 'public' draws attention to their use in both subjects, reinforcing students' understanding and helping them to apply their knowledge in different contexts, which reduces its fragility. By

---

57.   https://primarytimery.com/2017/10/28/the-3d-curriculum-that-promotes-remembering/
58.   https://holocaustlearning.org.uk/latest/the-problem-with-the-boy-in-the-striped-pyjamas/

doing so, we move towards effective and meaningful interdisciplinarity that reinforces students' understanding of each subject and draws attention to the symbiotic relationship between literature and history, which reinforces disciplinary knowledge in both.

The example of history and English explores the ideals of cross-subject collaboration; a lack of interdisciplinary cooperation in other subjects can be far more problematic. Both science and geography draw on the language and procedures of mathematics, whether for drawing graphs or calculating ratios and equations; yet rarely do departments collaborate on how these procedures are taught. In some cases, this lack of commonality around method or language is a requirement of the discipline and as always, we need to pay attention and be sensitive to this. There are also examples where the required processes for one subject contradict those required for another. In some maths examinations, specifications demand that students are taught to rearrange equations before then substituting in numbers, yet in science, students are expected to substitute first and then rearrange. In each case, students can be penalised for not following the specified method. Being aware of these contradictions and conflicts allows us to draw attention to them and pre-empt misconceptions or misapplication.

In addition, where an absence of interdisciplinary collaboration is more due to lack of cooperation between subjects than a disciplinary necessity, we can run the risk that students are asked to draw graphs or calculate equations through at least three different methods in three different subjects. Instead, through collaborative planning and deciding a common language for related procedures, we can reinforce students' understanding by activating prior knowledge from other subjects; reduce cognitive load as students repeat similar methods and procedures rather than expending time, energy and working memory attempting new methods for different subjects; and expose the interdisciplinary connections between subjects to reduce the fragility of students' knowledge through its application in different contexts.

To go further, we can look to the maths curriculum and consider how we can strengthen students' understanding of mathematical procedures when applied to other subjects through cross-subject sequencing. With a careful weighing of the opportunity cost, it is likely beneficial to sequence the maths curriculum in such a way that key processes such as graph drawing are explicitly taught in maths first, where this is part of the core substantive knowledge of the maths curriculum, prior to this being applied in geography or science. In doing so, we can utilise the expertise and knowledge in the maths department to ensure these principles and procedures are securely taught in their disciplinary home, before their application in other subjects.

However, a crucial word of caution: meaningful interdisciplinarity can only be successful if subject leaders are not asked to dilute their curriculum in service to another subject. The need to cover graphs in science in Year 7 should not dictate that maths change their sequencing, their curriculum and therefore, in essence, change their subject – it is not maths for scientists, it is maths. A subject's curriculum should be the best version of itself, crafted over time, without interference or compromise. If matching the sequence of teaching across subjects creates this interference, its utility is lost as the opportunity cost is too far imbalanced.

- Which subjects lend themselves to meaningful interdisciplinarity?
- Where can common language and methodology be used to reinforce students' understanding within and across subjects?
- How does the sequencing of the curriculum in one subject have potential to reinforce understanding in another?

CHAPTER 5
ASSESSMENT

Now that we understand the differing forms of knowledge that exist within a subject discipline, and how this might serve to inform the choices that we make not only of what we teach but when we teach it, we can move towards a consideration of the assessment of what has been learned. When working with the curriculum as a model of progression, there is a call to take a more sustainable approach to the way in which we assess. Distancing ourselves from throwaway termly assessments that claim to test skills yet check little more than the immediate knowledge of a unit, instead we would benefit to consider the way in which assessment acts as a measure for what has been taught, what has been learned and what we must do next. Taking an anticipatory approach to curriculum assessment, this chapter will outline how to move beyond haphazard assessment models of the past, so that we can build assessment systems which support the curriculum instead of distorting it.

Fragile knowledge

If our aim is for students to have a deep understanding of our subject, we need to recognise both when students have deep conceptual knowledge and when that knowledge is fragile. Fragile knowledge refers to when students do not understand, remember or consistently use what they have been taught, which results in an inability to successfully apply this knowledge independently and in different contexts. Fragile knowledge does not only refer to what students cannot remember after having been taught – it goes beyond the notion of knowledge that is simply 'missing'. Perkins asserts that the idea of knowledge being missing is too crude, positing that 'schooling minds is more than schooling memory.'[59] Rather, he uses the term fragile knowledge to include inert, naive and ritual knowledge.

Inert knowledge refers to students remembering information when tested, but not being able to apply it outside of those limited test conditions. A student can recall the principles of capitalism when quizzed in lesson but cannot apply this in an essay on *An Inspector Calls*; or they can parrot the equation for calculating volume but cannot apply this when presented with a problem that asks how many litres can be held in a container. This form of fragile knowledge is important to our understanding of how we move from shallow to deep understanding. To address this fragility, our curriculum needs to include explicit and systematic opportunities to harness prior knowledge – activating previous learning to inform new learning. Careful sequencing of our curriculum can clearly assist in this endeavour.

However, to go further than simple acquisition of knowledge, we need to address the issue of fragility and move our students towards judicious application. This ambition takes us beyond the 'pub-quiz curriculum' where students can only recall facts by rote, and takes us towards deeper understanding that focuses not only on possessing knowledge, but also being able to apply, synthesise, evaluate, connect and debate this knowledge in different contexts.

- How can our curriculum sequencing help to avoid fragile knowledge?
- Where can we find meaningful opportunities for students to apply knowledge?
- How can our assessment design identify and address this fragility?

Meaningful assessment

When the curriculum is defined and sequenced with care and attention paid to the types of knowledge in our subject, assessment design can be far more precise. Effective assessment is granular: it identifies the specific knowledge students have learnt and can apply, it pinpoints misconceptions,

---

59.   Perkins, D. (1995) *Smart Schools: From Training Memories to Educating.* Free Press.

and it is incremental. In some schools, the focus of assessment can become skewed towards an attempt to display progress – at times arbitrarily and at others falsely. However, if 'the curriculum is the progression model',[60] rather than attempt to apply levels or descriptors to 'demonstrate progress', our assessment needs to be finely tuned to identify how far each aspect of the curriculum has been mastered and where misconceptions must be addressed before moving to the next stage.

Soderstrom's principle of learning versus performance is key to our decisions around assessment:

> Learning refers to relatively permanent changes in knowledge or behavior. It is – or at least should be – the goal of education. Performance, on the other hand, refers to temporary fluctuations in knowledge or behavior that can be measured or observed during (or shortly after) instruction.[61]

We need to ensure that a student's response is indicative of what has been learnt, not what has been performed. Performance can create a facade for the teacher; a false sense of what has been understood and how durable that understanding is. Consequently, our assessment model must systematically probe at learning, not performance.

Granular assessment

A granular approach to assessment is required to identify with precision how successfully students have retained, understood and can apply what they have been taught. However, in many schools, assessment often relies on long-form essays or full exam papers. Whilst it may be effective in the sciences and maths to use exam papers to identify students' understanding, a summative essay in more cumulative subjects with students writing full essays or completing full papers every few weeks in order to assess progress

---

60. Fordham, M. (2020) 'What did I mean by "the curriculum is the progression model?"', https://clioetcetera. com/2020/02/08/what-did-i-mean-by-the-curriculum-is-the-progression-model/.
61. Soderstrom, N. C. & Bjork, R. A. (2015) 'Learning versus performance: An integrative review', *Perspectives on Psychological Science*, 10, 176–199.

is unlikely to be a useful method of assessment or, more importantly, to help students improve. When we assess holistically in this way, it is more difficult to home in on the precise areas that need to be reviewed, retaught and deliberately practised, and more difficult to identify what has been learnt to allow us to adjust our curriculum accordingly.

Identifying misconceptions

In order to assess what students know and can do with precision, we can look to multiple-choice quizzes (MCQs), which have become increasingly popular in schools. A well-structured MCQ can be extremely powerful, both in terms of identifying what students know and in addressing misconceptions. Our holistic assessment methods are less likely to offer this precision as misconceptions are more likely to be missed if the task or student does not explicitly refer to the aspects of the curriculum where these misconceptions lie.

Daisy Christodoulou,[62] by expanding on the work of Dylan Wiliam,[63] provides excellent advice on how to structure multiple-choice questions. Christodoulou suggests avoiding using answers that are obviously incorrect and instead designing questions with answers that are plausible but still unambiguously wrong. In addition, not telling students how many correct answers there are significantly reduces the likeliness of guesswork. However, for novice learners or those at the early stage of study, providing the number of possible answers to begin with can be used as a scaffold to help access the question and avoid cognitive overload.

Although clearly a useful tool for testing substantive knowledge, MCQs can also be used to assess students' disciplinary and procedural knowledge, allowing the teacher to test students' understanding of not only the content but also how to apply it, before they attempt or re-attempt an extended piece of work. This approach means issues can be addressed before students move to the next stage, and their errors and misconceptions can

---

62. Hendrick, C. & Macpherson, R. (2017) *What Does this Look Like in the Classroom? Bridging the Gap Between Research and Practice.* Woodbridge: John Catt.
63. Ibid.

be more sharply identified rather than having to be untangled from an extended piece. For instance, an essay on the causes of World War II might not expose a misunderstanding of the Treaty of Versailles, as a student may either choose to exclude it from their argument or simply parrot its inclusion without understanding what it means. Whereas a succinct multiple-choice question offers an efficient way to identify this type of misunderstanding, allowing the teacher to promptly address this and ensure knowledge is secured so the student can move forward.

In addition, the process of designing MCQs can be a particularly useful exercise for novice teachers as it draws attention to the possible misconceptions students may have and how to both plan for and address these.

For example, the Year 7 question below helps to identify the common misconception that 'lovely' is an adverb (due to its 'ly' suffix), and at the same time requires the student to be able to identify adjectives by process of elimination. The question therefore asks more of the student than just the definition and identification of an adverb.

Which of the following sentences include an adverb?

1. *Romeo and Juliet is one of Shakespeare's best-known plays.*
2. *The language used in the play is beautifully lyrical.*
3. *The two young protagonists quickly fall in love.*
4. *Lord Capulet is adamant that his lovely daughter will marry the suitor he has chosen for her.*
5. *The Prologue forewarns the audience that the play will end tragically.*

The Year 10 *Macbeth* question in the example below allows for interesting discussions surrounding blame whilst offering an opportunity for retrieval practice of the plot. When thoughtfully designed, these questions lend themselves to further elaboration and can offer a springboard for analysis or evaluation that take students beyond retrieval and towards a more detailed understanding.

Which of the following characters are killed at the hands of Macbeth?

1. *Banquo*
2. *King Duncan*
3. *Lady Macbeth*
4. *Macduff*
5. *Macdonwald*

To further increase the effectiveness of this form of assessment and to help students better respond to feedback, research by Stock et al suggests that the use of confidence scores can encourage a hypercorrection effect which will help students to learn from any mistakes they may have made.[64] When completing MCQs, students can be asked to add a confidence score of 1–5 for each question, with 1 indicating that the student is absolutely confident of their answer and 5 being not confident at all.

What similarities are there between ancient Greek and Mesopotamian civilisations?

1. *They were both based around a large river.*
2. *They were both centred around water.*
3. *They both traded with other civilisations.*
4. *They both grew large surpluses of wheat.*
5. *They both founded overseas colonies.*

How confident are you of your answer? 1 = not confident, 5 = very confident.	

If students find that a question they gave a confidence score of 1 for is incorrect, they are more likely to learn the correct answer to that question due to the hypercorrection effect. To enhance this further and more specifically address the misconceptions that resulted in the incorrect answers, students

---

64. Stock, W. A., Kulhavy, R. W., Pridemore, D. R. & Webb, J. M. (in press) 'Retrieving Responses and Confidence Estimates for Multiple-Choice Questions', *British Journal of Psychology*.

can be asked, when appropriate, to write next to their confidence score why they have chosen this answer. This approach allows the teacher to better understand and address where the misconceptions have arisen.

Encouraging flexibility

To move students from fragile knowledge to deep understanding, we need to ensure they have opportunities to apply their learning. As Young points out, too much focus on memorisation, although an 'integral part of any successful learning [...] is not an end in itself' and students need to be encouraged to 'develop a relationship to knowledge'.[65] To develop this relationship, the questions we ask should require elasticity of knowledge. As such, our assessments need to test and encourage flexibility. Questions which require rote repetition of facts or quotations will be less effective than those that allow students to demonstrate meaning, to transfer knowledge to new contexts or to make connections. This can be achieved, to an extent, through the questions we ask when quizzing, but we also need to take students beyond this into more flexible, meaningful and complex application.

Although long-form assessments should be spaced quite far apart to give students the opportunity to accumulate the knowledge and understanding needed to tackle them effectively, students need other opportunities to apply their knowledge to increasingly complex or extended tasks or in increasingly complex or sophisticated ways. The form this takes is dependent on the subject discipline; assessments that allow students to demonstrate their knowledge and understanding will never look the same in every subject. The best form of assessment will allow students to demonstrate what they know and can do in a way that is sensitive and appropriate to the subject discipline and the stage of the curriculum.

For instance, English, history, religious education or geography may all be assessed through an essay-based task, but the form and construction

---

65. Young. M, 'From Powerful Knowledge to the Powers of Knowledge', in C. Sealy & T. Bennet (eds.), *The researchED Guide to the Curriculum*. John Catt.

of these essays and their application of knowledge will be very different. Whilst English might provide the opportunity for a developed exploration of a text that invites the inclusion of criticism, geographical evaluation will often provide a clear, more rigid framework for both sides of the debate.

In a similar way, analysis in history takes a very different form to that in English, which needs to be explicitly taught: lending ideas between subjects for writing this form of assessment will only be useful to a very limited point and, as always, the discipline is king. However, subject leads should seek out how other subjects interpret assessment methodology – this is fundamental to understanding where assessment literacy can be utilised from other disciplines. Equally, we should identify where it is essential to stay faithful to our subject's own assessment literacy to ensure that it is taught in the bespoke way that is necessary for success within the subject.

- Effective assessment is granular.
- Multiple-choice questions allow precise identification of misconceptions.
- Assessment needs to be focused on learning and not performance.
- Application is required for students to demonstrate their understanding and move away from fragile knowledge.

CHAPTER 6
INSTRUMENTS OF THE CURRICULUM

As knowledge is selected, ordered and scrutinised to ensure it is fit for purpose and deserving of its place, we must then consider how we present this to our students in such a way that it is loyal to our curriculum aims. In practical terms, we need to design systems and materials that pay service to the curriculum but are also responsive to teachers and to students. These instruments of curriculum should develop the skill and knowledge of our teachers to liberate rather than stifle them, and should develop our learners in the same way.

The way we package our curriculum for delivery affects the way teachers and students regard it, and should move us beyond time laboured over animated PowerPoints or an abundance of worksheets. By creating effective curriculum materials for students, we can focus teacher time not on one-off time fillers, but products that have longevity and cohesion, which serve to develop the teacher as well as teach the student. Our key aim should be a quest for elegance in the implementation of the curriculum through our careful thinking around structure, substance and simplicity, so that we provide an enriching and meaningful enactment of the curriculum for both teachers and students.

Thinking, not doing

As Mary Myatt affirms, 'materials should privilege thinking over task completion.'[66] If we are to deliver curricular content in a way that is respectful to the subject discipline, then there needs to be an

---

66.   Myatt, M. (2019), 'Useful and beautiful', accessed at https://marymyatt.com/blog/2019-04-20/useful-and-beautiful.

understanding, particularly at classroom level, that time must be given generously to conceptualisation and contextualisation. Rob Coe asserts that learning takes place 'when people have to think hard,'[67] and such a process cannot be hurried, especially when building the foundations for meaningful conceptualisation to take place.

For example, students cannot fully understand photosynthesis without understanding both the macro and micro structure of plants. For this, they need to understand what plants need and how they access it. They therefore need to understand, to some extent, the process of chemical reaction (reactant + reactant → product). If students fail to grasp one step of this process, they will struggle to understand the next. Students need room to articulate this understanding and each stage within it. Very little of this process requires students to outline their thinking in writing, because the work is in making sense of such concepts before committing it to paper.

To support our students in conceptualising or making sense of our subject, we need to consider where we linger for longer: where time is devoted to thinking, and unpacking, and interpreting. When we anticipate where misconceptions may arise in planning our curriculum and its delivery, is this translated to our allocation of time for students to think hard and untangle these misconceptions with us? Put simply, where in our curriculum do we prioritise thought over task?

The materials we use to support the delivery of the curriculum should therefore offer the space for thinking and not just doing. Prescriptive resources, boxed sections for completing tasks, and overly detailed and structured booklets that restrict and confine our students' thinking, do not allow either the student or teacher to meaningfully engage with the curriculum. These materials can create a reliance that stifles both teacher and student development and reduces the curriculum to a list of tasks

---

67. Coe, R. (2013) 'Improving Education: a Triumph of Hope over Experience', Inaugural Lecture at Durham University, 18th June 2013.

to be worked through rather than a satisfying exploration of the subject. However, when workbooks are well-designed and used judiciously, they can offer a long-term, high-impact strategy for effectively implementing the curriculum.

Design

There is an essential caveat to any workbook design: it must pay service to the subject. For workbooks to be fit for purpose for both the teacher and the student, they must meet the needs of the discipline. Genericism is dangerous, and we would be wise to consider that one instrument of practice will never be the overarching sole model for all disciplines. There is no one format or template that can be faithful to all subjects; the subject informs how we present it to students. Cross-subject generic templates, fussy design, overly restrictive content, time-stamped tasks and excessive scripting can stifle the curriculum, the teacher and the student. In the most extreme cases, teachers click through PowerPoint slides or rely on annotated scripts without engaging with or being empowered by the subject material itself. Equally, there is a risk of misinterpretation, as the workbook is viewed as a replacement for knowledge. To do so results in somewhat of a failing for the workbook to achieve its purpose. Instead, workbooks can only ever act as a successful addition to the classroom, when accompanied by a teacher who seeks to develop themselves as an expert of the subject itself.

When workbooks do support the successful enactment of the curriculum, their benefits are manifold: they can reduce workload through centralised planning; they can offer structure and familiarity to both staff and students; they can make explicit the key foci for the curriculum; and in their most effective form, they can become much more than a pre-printed booklet of worksheets, and instead act as a vessel to lead and communicate curricular thinking. Whilst initially labour intensive, once established, workbooks can act as a tool to not only drive learning within the classroom in a cohesive, concise manner, but can also support teacher subject discourse and development in use within departmental meeting time, acting as the central focus for conversation and collaboration. By making choices around design that do not appeal to aesthetics, but encourage the actualisation of the subject itself, the workbook can then be used as a means of development, and not of confinement.

Therefore, the design of the workbook at a departmental level should be agreed and established by the specialists of the subject, who have a developed insight of how their subject should be created or actualised on the page. They will be able to ascertain the common language of their subject to use explicitly with students; where to be mindful of cognitive overload in respect to the content and its complexities; and where exemplar material will be most valuable. The design uses the discipline as a director, at all times.

Cohesive

For the teacher, the workbook acts as a dress pattern. It gives form to what we teach but allows a skilled specialist to embellish, create patterns and add rich details, to translate it into something meaningful in the classroom. In the words of Mayer, 'it gives you what you want, when you want it, rather than everything you could want, even when you don't.'[68] The workbook needs to present content in manageable chunks, carefully sequenced to mirror curricular intention. The workbook should naturally follow the hierarchies of the subject, helping to move students through ideas, concepts and applications in a logical way that tells them something of the structures of the subject itself. Oliver Caviglioli describes this as an example of 'architecture meet[ing] behaviourism':[69] as the design mirrors the underlying architecture of the subject, students develop an understanding of the subject through the format and design itself.

The workbook can therefore make visible the connections between fragments of knowledge and episodic lessons as students see concepts

---

68. Quoted in Whitbread, D. (2009) *The Design Manual.* NewSouth Publishing.
69. Caviglioli, O. 'Designing your book', accessed at https://static1.squarespace.com/static/58e151c946c3c418501c2f88/t/5b631ab988251bd3c40511e0/1533221569750/Designing+Your+Book.pdf.

introduced, explained, applied, revisited and repeated in new contexts through its deliberate sequencing. This provides a sense of cohesion by directing students to where they have seen concepts, vocabulary or models before, making visible their existing schema by exposing the connections between their past and present learning. For instance, students may be directed back to sustainability within the Sahara as they study the impact of natural environmental change in Antarctica, or revisit the definition of depicting a character as Machiavellian from their study of Juliet, as she outwits all but herself, as they begin to examine the character of Macbeth at a later point in their curriculum journey. A well-designed workbook is the product of deliberate curriculum choices and provides a vehicle for its effective enactment, through a loyalty to the conceptual.

Active

Workbooks typically demand an active participant; they do not act to replace or remove the teacher or student from their relationship with the subject. Sometimes misconstrued as an instrument for the idle, workbooks are produced as a labour of love. They offer teachers a starting point for enacting the curriculum by making explicit the translation from scheme of work to lesson material, to help teachers identify where their time is best directed in the lesson and in their own development of subject knowledge. As a consequence, teachers are liberated to spend time working collaboratively with others to discuss, review, evaluate and refine their delivery of the material itself rather than the making of it. However, the creation of workbooks is difficult because it exposes what we do not know. From an initial mapping out of the knowledge required, to deciding on what will feature and how student time will be spent, to identifying where students should be active or prioritise thinking, to the creation of materials and their use within the classroom, to the evaluation of where misconceptions have appeared, or to where our subject may have evolved and where this should be acknowledged – every stage of the process demands that we identify and then close gaps in our own subject knowledge.

Equally, the workbook should demand active student participation. Tasks posed as questions; an insistence on recalling of prior knowledge or plotting connections; securing procedural knowledge through process mapping, concise problem-solving or succinct note taking – these all help develop independence in students. Far from encouraging a lazy learner, the workbook offers scholarly engagement, not just in our subject but in what it means to study.

Valued

For an object to be valuable, it should have both utility and elegance. For us to create classroom materials that are held in high regard, we need to take their design seriously and handle their content with care. The workbook needs to be worthy of being central to our teaching. Preserving the value of the workbook requires continual review and refinement. However, this may not be achieved through simply adding more and more content. John Franklin stated 'Simplicity, carried to the extreme, becomes elegance', and the same principle is true here: the workbook should aim to support the teacher not through addition after addition, but instead by an intrepid process of simply considering what must be taught, and what must be discarded.

This need for simplicity is by no means aesthetic: elegance in design seeks to enable learners to access knowledge through a model that does not result in cognitive overload. Historically, challenge and depth has at times been misinterpreted as merely more information, leading to crammed pages of knowledge, plucked from a variety of sources with good intentions but poor consequences. Stripping the content of a workbook back to the necessary, back to the finest elements required to encourage discourse around the subject, provides an effective framework without overloading the teacher or student.

Finally, the workbook is collectively valued as central to the evolution of curriculum itself. It acts as a catalyst for discussion, bringing a team together to consider how to build upon the strengths that already exist and to edit, elaborate and refine. The fulfilling aspect of this work is that through discourse around the use of these materials, staff improve as a natural consequence. Departmental meetings can be used, workbook in hand, to plot out the week ahead- anticipating misconceptions, deliberating over quality of content, or even scripting questions to capture those pivotal moments for discussion. In the fullness of time, the workbook is just a prompt for meaningful talk that consequently drives the gradual yet powerful transformation of the curriculum.

- Create materials that frame the curriculum, not confine it.
- Demand an active participant through effective design.
- Compose workbooks that convey value for both teacher and student.

SECTION THREE: IN THE CLASSROOM
CUSTODIANS OF THE CURRICULUM

As a classroom teacher, knowing little more about the curriculum than what is outlined on a Word document handed to you in September, is both daunting and disempowering. Yet, historically, the design and development of the curriculum has been the business of only the few, as opposed to the responsibility of all. However, curriculum work is a teacher's work. As detailed in the Ofsted Teacher wellbeing research report, if we wish to retain teachers, it is paramount that we create systems that promote and encourage the ' teachers' belief that teaching is worthwhile.'[70] To feel a sense of ownership, involvement and engagement in what you teach is fundamental not only to your role as an effective teacher, but your sense of professional purpose within the classroom – meaningful curricular work offers exactly that. This section investigates the science, theory and practice of effective curriculum enactment, framing the role of the teacher as custodian of the curriculum.

---

70   Research and analysis *Summary and recommendations: teacher well-being research report*, 2019, accessed at https://www.gov.uk/government/publications/teacher-well-being-at-work-in-schools-and-further-education-providers/summary-and-recommendations-teacher-well-being-research-report

CHAPTER 7
RECLAIMING THE
ROLE OF THE TEACHER

Once we have wrangled with our vision for the curriculum, it is over to the teacher to translate it for their students. Yet often in schools, curriculum enactment is engineered and mandated from the top down. If you are 'just' a teacher, your role is merely an act of delivery, with little autonomy or involvement with the content itself, or how it came to be designed. Even if this arrangement is attributed to the noble intention of reducing workload, with curriculum design undertaken by a select few within a department, the enforced relinquishment of the classroom teacher's proprietary role as expert of their subject has resulted in them leaving the profession or being dissatisfied in school roles. With the best of intentions, by over-resourcing the curriculum, schools can deskill teachers.

Crawford et al. differentiate between two types of demand: challenge demands, which 'have the potential to promote mastery, personal growth or future gains', and hindrance demands, which 'have the potential to thwart personal growth, learning and goal attainment'.[71] If we do not balance the scales by reducing 'hindrance demands' and removing those aspects of the teacher's role that do not add impact or value to what we do, our enjoyment of teaching as well as our efficacy and effectiveness is

---

71.   Crawford, E. R., LePine, J. A. & Rich, B. L. (2010) 'Linking job demands and resources to employee engagement and burnout: A theoretical extension and meta-analytic test', *Journal of Applied Psychology*, 95 (5), 834–848.

likely to be significantly reduced. At the same time, we need to increase our focus on 'challenge demands' that allow us to flex our professional and intellectual muscles. The curriculum, with its reliance on intellectual debate, subject expertise and skilled implementation can offer these challenge demands and in doing so, offer teachers a sense of purpose and satisfaction that may otherwise be lost.

- Engaging in challenging meaningful tasks offers professional satisfaction.
- We should look to reduce hindrance demands and increase challenge demands in what we ask of our teachers.

Autonomy and purpose

According to the NFER study of teacher autonomy, 'teachers report relatively low autonomy over assessment and feedback, pupil data collection and curriculum content'.[72] This has contributed to teachers continuing to leave the profession, and leaving it with complete disillusionment that the role was connected to their intellectual pursuit of their subject. If we are to re-engage teachers with this overarching sense of purpose, we must re-engage them with the essence of their subject specialism.

It could be argued that subject expertise and curriculum design have always been a priority for the classroom teacher, but that external factors have sought to change our direction or draw our attention to other things. While we have been party to debates around talk time, differentiation, assessment for learning, didactic teaching and collaborative learning, curriculum has sometimes been lost in the focus on pedagogy.

- Teachers leave because they are disappointed with the lack of autonomy.
- Autonomy and a balance of demands are essential to teachers' sense of purpose and job satisfaction.
- Curriculum is our tool to accomplish this.

---

72.   https://www.nfer.ac.uk/news-events/nfer-blogs/seven-new-insights-into-teacher-autonomy/

Subject expertise vs generic pedagogy

If we do not prioritise teachers' subject expertise or consider curriculum design as an inherent and inextricable part of their role, we can disempower teachers and fail to recognise their potential and value. This disconnection of the teacher from the subject can be partly attributed to the focus we take when training and developing teachers. More often than not, it is pedagogical theory and research that are the focus of professional development, and subject knowledge can become an afterthought or an expectation the teacher will address on their own. This results in an over-reliance on generic pedagogy that can be restrictive and counterintuitive, rather than on subject expertise and its vital role in informing its delivery. The question should never be either/or. Professional development must pay service to both in order to best equip our teachers.

- Our focus needs to shift towards developing subject expertise rather than on generic pedagogical practices that can compromise the teaching of our subjects.

Inflexible to flexible delivery

A focus on subject expertise also empowers us to move away from rigid structures and practices. Effective curriculum delivery and prioritising subject expertise requires us to move away from *inflexible planning* – that is, minute-by minute planning of tasks and questions – towards *flexible planning* led by powerful knowledge and key learning moments that we become more familiar with as we progress towards the status of expert teacher. If we spent more time on curriculum and subject expertise than pedagogical practice, our delivery would be far more purposeful and pay greater service to the subject as a result. This is mirrored in the findings by Ofsted in their investigation into how to assess the quality of education through curriculum intent, implementation and impact, where they identify that 'staff subject knowledge was of considerable importance, particularly when it came to designing appropriate progression through content'.[73]

Are we training teachers in an inflexible way that focuses on pedagogy rather than subject as a means of rapidly preparing them for their almost immediate introduction to the classroom? As they become more accomplished over time, do they shed this inflexibility for a more malleable, autonomous approach? If so, our continued development of teachers needs to be mindful of this 'unshedding' and thus presents the real challenge[74]: it calls for a remodelling and refocusing of our approach to teacher development and training that is far more challenging than sharing one-size-fits all practices, and requires a move towards a deep, intellectual pursuit of subject knowledge and the means to facilitate this.

- We need to support teachers in moving from inflexible to flexible planning through subject-based training.

Reframing the role of teacher

We know that 'a teacher who had been teaching at a particular grade level for more than five years is positively and significantly associated with increased student achievement,'[75] but this continual improvement plateaus somewhat after these five years.[76] However, if we can reframe what it means to be a teacher by developing subject expertise, and by enriching our curriculum and its teaching as a result, we can work to avoid this plateau and reinvigorate our profession. Christine Counsell puts this well:

73. Ofsted (2018), *An investigation into how to assess the quality of education through curriculum intent, implementation and impact,* accessed at https://assets.publishing.service.gov.uk/government/uploads/system/uploads/attachment_data/file/766252/How_to_assess_intent_and_implementation_of_curriculum_191218.pdf.

74. Nickerson, R. S. (1998) 'Confirmation Bias: A Ubiquitous Phenomenon in Many Guises', *Review of General Psychology,* 2 (2), 175–220.

75. Metzler, J. & Woessmann, L. (2012) 'The Impact of Teacher Subject Knowledge on Student Achievement: Evidence from Within-Teacher Within-Student Variation', *Journal of Development Economics,* 99 (2), pp. 486–496.

76. Danielson, C. (2007), *Enhancing professional practice: A framework for teaching.* Association for Supervision and Curriculum Development.

I love being around secondary teachers who are well trained, very well read and who are up on the debate because they're all just very humble: how can we do better? How do you do it? It has a profound effect on well-being.[77]

By being involved in curriculum development through a collaborative process of discussion around what it should and could look like when translated to the classroom, teachers feel a true sense of purpose in their day-to-day work which, within the wider educational climate, can do nothing but improve both the retention of teachers and the quality of education overall.

- Our reframing of the role of the teacher as subject expert can support both retention and the quality of education.

---

77. Interview with Kat Howard and Christine Counsell, July 2019.

CHAPTER 8
CURRICULUM IN ACTION

For teachers to be effective in their role as custodians of the curriculum, both individually and as part of a collegiate, they must be supported in a thorough comprehension of what this means once curriculum is translated within a classroom setting. For the curriculum to be effective in action, teachers must be able to work beyond the blueprint of schemes of work or shared resources and engage with the complexities of curriculum delivery – from understanding how their own expertise can both strengthen and hinder their delivery, to anticipating misconceptions, to leading learning through rigorous enquiry. Our curriculum is much more than a document or a set of PowerPoints, and it requires knowledge and expertise for it to be enacted successfully.

Curse of the expert

We need to be aware that developing expertise in a subject can come with a problematic side-effect: Heath et al. propose that 'once we know something, we find it hard to imagine what it's like not to know it.'[78] Experts endanger the teaching of their subject through either struggling to break down the components of their subject to make the abstract more concrete for students, or by failing to communicate the subtle stages required for learning because these are second nature to them.

Where expert teachers do prosper is in their ability to draw from vast mental models to consider where they have encountered the issue before, how they responded in that moment, how successful the action they took was, and how it might be refined for the current situation. As we develop

---

78.   Heath, D. & Heath, C. (2008) *Made to Stick: Why some ideas take hold and others come unstuck.* Arrow.

expertise and knowledge within our subject, it is pertinent to remember our novice students and plan our teaching to accommodate them: we must ensure that our curriculum takes our students with us at every step and that we do not forget what it is like to be a novice.

There will be times when we need to consciously act against our own 'second nature' approach by working to disassemble and reassemble the component parts required for learning in our subject. We need to consider what these components will look like, how learners will encounter them and what might be refined to improve this experience for a novice. We need to use our expertise to anticipate where learners are most likely to encounter difficulty within our subject, but more importantly, why it is at this particular moment that students struggle, even when it seems natural to us. We then need to package this for students in such a way that it reduces or avoids these difficulties rather than reinforces them. We need to work hard to ensure that this curse does not hinder the work we do as teachers and attempt to eradicate the bias of expert in the classroom.

- How do we prepare for what we know to be the stumbling blocks of our subject?
- Where do we make concrete the terminology for our subject, to which we are so familiar?
- How do we keep in mind what it is like to be a novice of our subject?

Anticipating misconceptions

A key benefit of subject expertise is in pre-empting the misconceptions that arise frequently in our subject. All students bring misconceptions to the classroom and these 'arise from students' prior learning, either in the classroom (especially for mathematics) or from their interaction with the physical and social world', which we could not hope to control outside of our school remit.[79] Learning in action is therefore a case of doing and undoing what has come before.

---

79. Smith, J. P., diSessa, A. A. & Roschelle, J. (1993) 'Misconceptions Reconceived: A Constructivist Analysis of Knowledge in Transition Author(s)', *The Journal of the Learning Sciences*, 3 (2), 115–163.

Through their immersion in the subject, teachers can begin to collate an extensive bank of misconceptions that students are likely to bring to the classroom as a result of prior learning and experience. If this process is planned beforehand, and as so many of the misconceptions that we encounter are common ones, we can begin to predict where students may stumble. By identifying what we want students to learn and working backwards to identify where each stumbling block may arise, we can ensure we sequence teaching in such a way that these misconceptions may be avoided. We can also explicitly draw students' attention to these misconceptions or pitfalls, and through hypercorrection, detailed explanation and careful modelling, reduce the likelihood of them being repeated by our students. Finally, we can ensure we have efficient methods for identifying these misconceptions so they can be promptly addressed.

These skilful methods of planning, delivery and assessment require deep subject knowledge on behalf of the teacher. Collaborative planning and engagement with high-quality subject communities can meaningfully provide subject knowledge development by drawing on the collective expertise within and across schools.

A forensic approach to breaking down key concepts to identify where misconceptions may arise is also an effective approach to planning. Take for example subtraction at primary level. To understand how to subtract a two-digit number from a two-digit number, primary students need to know:

Place value rules	Partitioning across and within ten	Bonds of numbers within ten	Knowledge of the number system as linear

Students are likely to fall foul of thinking that both numbers can be partitioned for subtraction as they can be for addition: 32 + 26 can be 30 and 20 and 2 and 6. However, this is not the case for subtraction: 30 − 20 = 10, but subtracting 6 from 2 will not provide the correct answer, because the process is not applicable here. If we do not teach the components laid out with an awareness of what is likely to create misconceptions along the way, the chances of such shortcomings are increased.

To ensure students have a secure understanding of concepts and processes, as well as their pitfalls, exclusions and exceptions, we must consider how each of these examples and non-examples will be addressed as this is where our misconceptions will most likely lie. This explicit focus on misconceptions reduces the time taken to make adjustments or corrections and secures better student understanding as a result. We know that 'practice makes permanent' and so the less our students practise their misconceptions, the easier they are to undo or avoid.

- What are the common misconceptions and misunderstandings in our subject?
- Where does our curriculum delivery actively seek these out?

Learning through enquiry

Soderstrom affirms that '*learning* refers to relatively permanent changes in knowledge or behaviour [whereas] *performance* refers to temporary fluctuations in knowledge or behaviour that can be measured.'[80] We need to move past the idea that if students are 'doing' they must be 'learning', which we can fall foul of if we limit our curriculum to learning objectives. Where learning requires changes in knowledge and behaviour over time, a focus on learning objectives can be a hindrance as they often employ the language of examinations and can manipulate 'learning' as a result. Presenting learning as an action that can be accomplished within an isolated lesson, without need of revisit or refinement, is highly misleading. To present curriculum learning as 'to know how to respond to a structure question' or 'to analyse a historical artefact' conforms to what Soderstrom describes as 'performance'. It carries the implication that after a 60-minute lesson, students will be able to 'understand/apply/create/evaluate,' rather than assert what they know and can apply over time.

---

80. Soderstrom, N. & Bjork, R. (2015) 'Learning Versus Performance: An Integrative Review. Perspectives on Psychological Science', *Association for Psychological Science*, 10, 176–199.

Objectives driven by the language of declarative knowledge can also be misleading. It is not possible for students to 'know number bonds to ten' after one lesson because this statement discounts the foundation of knowledge, practice and application over time required to achieve this aim. It is therefore unhelpful to plan learning around an either/ or objective based on knowledge vs. skills or declarative vs. procedural knowledge; our planning for learning needs to incorporate both in a way that acknowledges these accumulate over time.

Enquiry over objectives offers a potential solution to this issue. This is not to be confused with 'inquiry learning' that takes the form of minimally guided instruction that 'ignore[s] the structures that constitute human cognitive architecture.'[81] The enquiry approach ensures that teaching focuses on the knowledge required for students to gain a level of expertise over time. This shift from skill to expertise,[82] unlike learning objectives, recognises that skills do not exist in isolation and are a manifestation of knowledge in practice. Reshaping learning through enquiry by leading with well-designed questions has the effect of driving learning within and across lessons. This way, students can be inducted into the vast ideas of our subjects and then articulate their own interpretation of those ideas within a framework that lends itself to their application. This offers a more secure understanding of learning over time, rather than isolated performance.

- Learning objectives can hinder the student experience, manipulate learning, and imply that skills can be learned and permanently retained through single-lesson teaching.
- Learning through enquiry offers a flexible approach towards students gaining expertise over time through a synthesis of knowledge and application.

---

81. Kirschner, P. A., Sweller, J. & Clark, R. E. (2006) 'Why minimal guidance during instruction does not work: An analysis of the failure of constructivist, discovery, problem-based, experiential, and inquiry-based teaching', *Educational Psychologist*, 41 (2), 75–86.
82. See 'There is no dichotomy', page 44

Enquiry questions

Enquiry questions can enable students to consider the big questions of our subjects. A far cry from references to skills or assessment objectives, enquiry questions provide us with a strategic direction for accumulating and applying the substance of our curriculum. For example, the learning objective:

> *Upon completing this assignment, students will be able to provide accurate diagrams of cells and be able to classify cells from microscopic images.*
> …becomes:
> *What is the structure of a living organism?*

To take a further example:

> *To produce a drawing using a series of different examples by Kandinsky, using oil-based materials.*
> …becomes:
> *How did Kandinsky contribute to the art world?*

This robust enquiry ensures that learning is driven by a focus on conceptual thinking, pulling at the contentions of our subject so that as we make our way through the curriculum, we return to the same big ideas, with new and existing knowledge connecting the threads that have accumulated over time. Instead of placing a focus upon a test, or narrow corner of learning over one or two lessons, enquiry questions seek to provide a vaster view of the discipline for the student.

As Counsell articulates, 'it is a way of knitting together a sequence of lessons in a powerful way'[83] instead of reverting to objectives that imply we can master the inner workings of our subject one cog at a time. Laying out lines of inquiry for both students and teachers provides clarity that it is

---

83.   Counsell, C. (2012), 'Building Powerful Enquiry Based Learning', https://andallthatweb.files.wordpress. com/2012/07/wrestling-with-enquiry-questions.pdf.

these big ideas that will help to bring form, direction and meaning to our thinking. If these questions are to support our enactment of a coherent curriculum through the connections and patterns they expose, they need to be actively called upon when we teach. The questions should not sit neglected on a whiteboard, or outlined on an overview document, but should help students to see their direction of travel and how what they are learning is connected by this enquiry, making visible their learning over time.

This approach allows students to apply their understanding meaningfully, by drawing together their knowledge to avoid a sense of learning as being fragmented, disjointed and unconnected. Enquiry questions allow students to apply all they have learnt, through questions that pay service to the discipline rather than through generic objectives guided by command words and not the subject itself.

Nevertheless, enquiry questions do not offer a quick fix for curriculum sequencing nor should they be employed as a generic approach to curriculum design. As always, our instruments for enacting the curriculum must pay service to the subject. Whilst such questions may offer fertile ground for many of our subjects, using enquiry questions as the basis for a maths curriculum, for example, is not appropriate for the discipline and is more likely to undermine the design of the curriculum than to enhance it. The strategies we employ must respond to the needs of the subject and place these front and centre, rather than attempt to roll out blanket approaches in a bid to provide simple solutions to complex issues which are wholly subject-specific.

- Enquiry questions offer strategic direction within and across lessons, avoiding fragmentation of knowledge.
- Enquiry questions support students' understanding by drawing together the threads of knowledge learnt over time and allowing them to apply this within a meaningful framework.

Vast and limitless learning

For enquiry questions to be effective, they need to incorporate the language of our subject and be intentional in their design so they open up possibilities for interpretation, contention and nuance that encourage flexible knowledge and meaningful understanding. If these are then complemented by our use of multiple-choice questions to ascertain what has been learnt, we can begin to triangulate how well students have mastered the curriculum.[84] If our enquiry questions do not encourage this flexibility and they limit how students can respond, we risk students mimicking what they have been told rather than demonstrating their understanding.

Furthermore, enquiry questions are central to scientific enquiry. To reduce curricular experience to a declarative objective such as 'to identify a monophyletic group' drives learning towards simple classification that undermines and restricts deep understanding – students are left with a haphazard grasp of a key biological classification that relies less upon critical enquiry and more on surface-level retention and reuse of the content covered. Reframing the enquiry as one where students question the significance of monophyletic groups to human beings exposes students to their ancestry and evolution. This builds stronger schematic frameworks by exposing students to the relationships and connections between organisms that form a substantive part of the subject discipline.

Similarly, the question 'To what extent is Macbeth a victim?' suggests that Macbeth's status as a victim is factual. Although the question stem looks to encourage debate or scale, the bias of the question has already seeded an interpretation. This framing shifts the student's role from critic back to conduit of knowledge. By directing them towards one line of inquiry, rather than contemplating the complexity of the character, they might then fail to consider the other aspects of his character, or the themes he might represent. Instead, asking 'Who is Macbeth?' allows students to draw on their own knowledge and interpretation and take these in different directions to demonstrate their understanding and the threads

---

84. See 'Assessment' page 77.

they have picked up, allowing students to think conceptually rather than parroting a given interpretation.

Our enquiry questions therefore need to encourage flexible knowledge from students, helping them to develop a deeper understanding and reducing knowledge fragility. They also ward against the false dichotomy of knowledge vs. skills through focus on expertise that ensures learning is led by the subject discipline and not reduced to generic performance.

Enquiry questions will and should look very different in different subjects and for different topics. They need to expose what students have learnt and can apply over time and this is unlikely to be achieved through generic question stems. The strength of our questions can be measured by whether they require a subject specialist to answer them; if they demand knowledge of the subject, it follows that they will require students to have engaged with and understood this knowledge to apply it to the question. Therefore, if enquiry questions are to be effective, they need to be designed in a way that is sensitive to the subject discipline.

- Enquiry-led learning encourages flexible knowledge and deep understanding.
- Enquiry questions need to be sensitive to the subject discipline and avoid genericism across topics and subjects.

CHAPTER 9
THE ROLE OF MEMORY

As both established and emerging research continues to indicate, cognitive science is integral to curriculum development. An understanding of memory function serves as a crucial tool to help teachers ensure that learning is permanent, thereby taking students beyond an ephemeral experience of the curriculum towards one that promotes a powerful change in their long-term memory.

Ebbinghaus' forgetting curve

To secure learning over time rather than as fleeting lesson performance, we can employ methods of retrieval to ensure a change has occurred in long-term memory. As proposed by Kirschner et al, 'if nothing has changed in long-term memory, nothing has been learned'.[85] Therefore, we need to look towards effective methods of achieving these changes. Ebbinghaus introduced the forgetting curve to illustrate how information could be recalled the same day at a rate of 100%, but this dropped to 40% after a few days, and continued to decline after that. Within seven days, without practice, retrieval was at a 0% success rate. Articulating to students the process of forgetting in order to recall information again later is essential to their knowledge of effective study practice, and allows teachers to reinforce conceptual connections from one episode of study to the next. Encouraging the art of forgetting and remembering ensures a higher likelihood of students being able to recall information and knowledge in the future.

---

85. Kirschner, P. A., Sweller, J. & Clark, R. E. (2006) 'Why minimal guidance during instruction does not work: An analysis of the failure of constructivist, discovery, problem-based, experiential, and inquiry-based teaching', *Educational Psychologist*, 41 (2), 75–86.

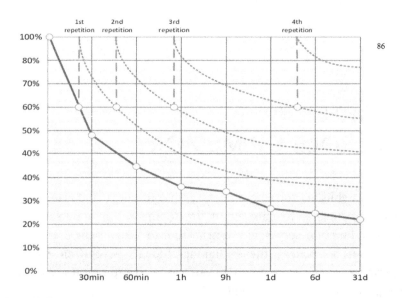

Utilising our understanding of memory helps to provide curriculum longevity because it reinforces learning as not simply covering content, but also ensuring there has been a 'change in long-term memory'. In doing so, we ensure our curriculum is valued for its long-term endurance rather than regarded as temporary or fleeting.

Activating prior knowledge

This process also provides students with a regular, habitual way of making connections between what has been learned before and what is being learned in the present. Activating prior knowledge and introducing new knowledge concurrently is one of the factors Ebbinghaus attributes to assisting in retention and recall of key knowledge previously learned.[87] To ensure that we use memory to our advantage when teaching curriculum content, we must plot out the connections that we hope to make between prior knowledge and that which is to be learnt.

---

86. Murre, J. M. J. & Dros, J. (2015) 'Replication and Analysis of Ebbinghaus' Forgetting Curve', *PLOS One*, 10 (7), https://doi.org/10.1371/journal.pone.0120644.

87. Explored in Paivio, A. (2013) 'Dual coding theory, word abstractness, and emotion: A critical review of Kousta et al.', *Journal of Experimental Psychology: General*, 142 (1), 282–287.

If we look to teach reproduction and variation before teaching the structure of a cell, then try to revisit one to connect to the other, our curriculum content becomes disjointed. Instead, to teach cells first means that when science teachers arrive at reproduction, they are able to test retrieval of cells to then develop expertise and outline the function of specialised cells. By making this explicit in our delivery, students are provided with a curriculum with coherence, plotted out with care, with logical connections between threads of knowledge from one to the next, which increases its permanence through retrieval and elaboration.

Reducing extraneous load

Activating prior knowledge also reduces cognitive load[88] by limiting the extraneous load[89] placed on working memory. In the classroom, the effects of cognitive overload may manifest in a student's inability to understand, make connections between or articulate what they have been taught. By accessing pre-existing knowledge, students' working memory is freed up to focus on and make connections to new material. However, the effectiveness of our instruction and the steps we take to reduce extraneous load can be undermined by ineffective resource design, unfamiliar vocabulary, attention-splitting by reading from a PowerPoint, or the classroom environment itself in terms of disruption in lessons or excessively busy classroom design. These contributors to extraneous load can affect how well students are able to understand new ideas and commit them to long-term memory.

Desirable difficulties

To further support students in committing ideas to long-term memory, we may rightly look towards 'desirable difficulties'.[90] The phrase, coined by Bjork, is used to define a task which requires significant effort but offers a reward to the learner through the challenge they offer and the effect this has on long

---

88. See 'Curriculum Sequencing' page 61.
89. Sweller, J. (1988), 'Cognitive Load During Problem Solving: Effects on Learning', *Cognitive Science*, 12, 257–285.
90. Bjork, R. A. (1994), 'Memory and metamemory considerations in the training of human beings', in J. Metcalfe & A. Shimamura (eds.), *Metacognition: Knowing about knowing.* Cambridge, MA: MIT Press.

term memory. Whilst these more challenging tasks take a longer time to complete, and require a considerable amount of effort, they are recognised as valuable by the student because of the challenge presented to them and by them. Desirable difficulties such as varying conditions of practice by asking students to apply knowledge in different forms and to different tasks to limit predictability; providing contextual interference by weaving in opportunities for knowledge recall outside of its original context; and distributing practice by spacing retrieval over time, can all act to improve cognitive strength. However, this can sometimes be a little haphazard in practice. As teachers look to leap back and forth between units of learning, students can get lost along the way as they attempt to make sense first of one idea, then the one before, then return again, with little awareness of the connections between them. Whilst this may improve the retrieval strength of knowledge, doing so in a way that creates fragmentation and disjointedness undermines the schematic webs required for deep understanding of the subject and the patterns and relationships of the knowledge that underpin it. This is why retrieval needs to promote flexible knowledge, whereby prior knowledge is activated with the explicit purpose of informing and reinforcing new learning.

The aim is to create meaningful connections between what is being learnt now and what has come before in a form best suited to what we want students to retrieve. Retrieval practice in the form of pre-scripted quizzes or a rigidly set number and structure of questions chosen at random for each lesson, irrespective of the context of the classroom, are unlikely to be effective as they are not responsive to the needs of the learner or to the curriculum itself. Where these questions are pre-planned based on activating the knowledge required for each stage of the curriculum, there is likely more benefit than randomly generated quiz questions, and it may well be efficient to have a bank of high-quality questions available for the department. However, if these are to be used, their selection should be based on the learning at hand and the level of the learner, rather than either selected at random or determined too far in advance.

Retrieval questions should also encourage flexible knowledge rather than repetition by rote. In English, once texts have been securely taught, spaced retrieval of students' knowledge of quotations is better utilised in exploring connections within and across texts than in simple parroting of phrases. Within *An Inspector Calls*, we can increase the utility of asking students to recall the Inspector's 'members of one body' speech by asking them to draw connections between this and Mr Birling's speech just before the Inspector's arrival. This retrieval task during the opening of a lesson exploring the use of exits and entrances in *Macbeth* helps to expose the disciplinary function of dramatic devices whilst offering an opportunity for effective retrieval.

Similarly, if our retrieval question were to ask students to simply define beta decay, we are likely to be met with regurgitation or mimicry that tells us little of students' conceptual understanding. If we reframe the question to ask how beta decay occurs, students then have to draw upon their knowledge of the placement of the neutron in the nucleus, that the breakdown of the neutron will result in the production of a proton and electron, and that the electron must exit the nucleus as a beta particle, leaving the proton in the nucleus as a result. They draw upon a far richer mental map of the process to consider not only their knowledge of beta decay, but also the sequence of processes and the relational qualities between each respective component. To take this further, if this retrieval was employed within a learning episode where students considered radioactive half-life, they could then apply this prior knowledge to help understand how long stable atoms could survive or how little time unstable atoms can endure radioactive decay. Articulating their understanding of half-life would likely be possible without this knowledge, but the conceptual connection of beta decay helps to inform students' knowledge to produce a more exacting response.

Through a nuanced and sensitive approach to these desirable difficulties, we remind students of the important moments in prior teaching, draw their attention to the relationships and patterns of our subject, and encourage the effective conceptual recall required to enhance their understanding of what will come next. As a consequence, knowledge is instilled safely within students' long-term memory, not as some sort of linear filing system, but as a latticework of knowledge, as we make conceptual connections between one interval and the next.

- Spaced retrieval practice helps secure knowledge in long-term memory.
- Activating prior knowledge can be used to reduce cognitive load.
- Varying conditions of practice, providing contextual interference and distributing practice on a given task can all act to improve cognitive strength.
- By coinciding the act of remembering with the introduction of new knowledge, we can enable students to make meaningful curricular connections.

CHAPTER 10
EXPLICIT INSTRUCTION

Whilst cognitive research highlights the benefits of regular retrieval and review, we also need to ensure that our initial instruction is guided by principles of research-informed practice. Our curriculum time is finite and so it is vital we look to how we can best use that time. Effective curriculum enactment requires the teacher to act as guardian and guide of the subject. We must pay heed to the work of Clark, Kirschner and Sweller, who offer a definitive argument for a teacher-guided approach to instruction within the classroom:

> Although unguided or minimally guided instructional approaches are very popular and intuitively appealing [...] these approaches ignore both the structures that constitute human cognitive architecture and evidence from empirical studies over the past half-century that consistently indicate that minimally guided instruction is less effective and less efficient than instructional approaches that place a strong emphasis on guidance of the student learning process.[91]

Without clear guidance through the tricky territory of our subject, it is easy for students to lose precious time in attempting to establish accurate knowledge through their own lines of inquiry rather than through effective instruction. Worse still, through a lack of subject custodianship on the teacher's behalf, students can be left to form repeated, engrained

---

91.   Clark, R. E., Kirschner, P. A. & Sweller, J. (2012) 'Putting Students on the Path for Learning: The Case for Fully Guided Instruction', *American Educator*, Spring 2012.

misconceptions through peer teaching; to engage in directionless discourse devoid of guidance or structure; or to undertake ineffective research that can tangle up their understanding of key issues. Even with the best of intentions, these pedagogical practices can damage students' conception of the subject. Equally, the metacognitive processes required to monitor our own knowledge, and to consider it in relation to what we do not yet know or are yet to understand, is no task for novice students to autonomously undertake.[92] Fully guided teacher instruction, when enacted effectively, can be an art-form in itself and requires high-quality planning and a focus on subject and pedagogical expertise.

Explicit curriculum delivery

The way we introduce new ideas to students can contribute to whether our curriculum flourishes or falters. From the vocabulary that we use to convey terms, to the way we present key moments for consideration or critique, our delivery must be constructed in such a way that it offers the best possible explanation of ideas and systematically seeks out what students do not understand. We need to furnish ourselves with ways of explaining curricular content that provides students with a narrative, enabling them to make connections between one moment and the next.

At subject level, the classroom teacher works as an integral part of the team to decide the common language of their subject, drawing on the experience and expertise of the department to wrangle with the best explanations for exploring key concepts. This becomes part of our in-house vocabulary, as we explore concepts with students using language that takes a 'no-shock' approach: students become familiar with how we refer to content in a way that is demanding, yet because they recognise it so frequently it becomes part of their own linguistic architecture.

To exemplify: students are introduced to the term 'imperialism' in their study of the British Empire, which they then revisit as a key cause of war

---

92. Tobias, S. & Everson, H. T. (2002) 'Knowing What You Know and What You Don't: Further Research on Metacognitive Knowledge Monitoring', CollegeBoard.

when they study World War I, before then considering theories of empire or New Imperialism at KS5. The vocabulary becomes embedded in how students discuss and understand the history, as we affirm: 'this is the language of our subject, and this is why.' When we later come to introduce New Imperialism at KS5, we may say: 'Previously, we looked at the way imperialism relied on territorial acquisition and the role of the armed forces. New Imperialism works more subtlety because it can exist at a local level, and without military interference.'

In this way, our delivery helps to create explicit connections for students and works as what is now ubiquitously referred to as a 'box set',[93] where episodes of new learning begin with a 'previously...' introduction, which draws attention to where this new learning lies within the overarching narrative of our subject as well as in its 'sub-plots', lesson by lesson or topic by topic. Willingham reinforces why drawing students' attention to the narrative arc of our curriculum is likely to be effective in students' understanding of it:

> The human mind seems exquisitely tuned to understand and remember stories – so much so that psychologists sometimes refer to stories as 'psychologically privileged.'[94]

Explanation of curriculum content should therefore be conveyed in such a way that it demystifies the subject for our students by exposing the threads that weave through it via the use of a common language across the curriculum that ties these threads together.

Using challenging subject-specific vocabulary therefore not only ensures we do not compromise on our use of disciplinary language, but also enables students to explicitly recognise the narrative that connects one stage of the curriculum to the next.

---

93. Almond, N. (2020), 'Curriculum Coherence', in C. Sealy & T. Bennet (eds.), *The researchED Guide to the Curriculum*. John Catt.
94. Willingham. D, (2010) *Why Don't Students Like School? A Cognitive Scientist Answers Questions About How the Mind Works and What It Means for the Classroom*. Jossey Bass.

Combining effective explanation of the hinterland[95] of our subject along with the connections within and between each episode of learning further draws on the power of narrative to create concrete, memorable experiences for students. Smith and Shortt articulate the importance of narrative:

> ...a story is more than a collection of timeless pieces of information because it moves from past to future, from memory to vision. It can therefore offer us not just individual items to consider, but a sense of direction, and orientation with time and history, an image of where we have come from and where we might be headed.[96]

Exposing the narratives of our subject and those formed by the curriculum itself gives more power to our explanation and delivery: stories linger, and are our memory's closest ally.

- Be intentional in using common language across your subject.
- Expose the narratives of your subject through this common language.
- Employ these stories to give direction and substance to what is being learnt.

Curriculum demonstration

When using models, we need to invest as much time in demonstrating the process as we do in showcasing the final outcome. Otherwise, where we hope to achieve a meaningful, concrete way of demonstrating success, students can simply feel overwhelmed and disheartened by the perceived gap between their current level and the final product. At best, we end up with poor imitations of the original model, and 'measures need to be taken to discourage unproductive imitation of exemplars.'[97] Done badly, modelling can hinder the enactment of our curriculum; we risk promoting

---

95. See 'Hinterland knowledge'.
96. Smith, D. & Shortt, J. (2015) quoted in Hannam, F. D. 'Teaching through Narrative', *Forum on Public Policy Online*.
97. Toa, J. & Carless, D. (2014) 'Making productive use of exemplars: Peer discussion and teacher guidance for positive transfer of strategies', *Journal of Further and Higher Education*, 40 (6), 746–764.

the application of knowledge as formulaic or prescriptive, which inhibits learning rather than enhancing it.[98]

If we regularly present students with examples without effective procedural instruction, we tend to find replicated not-quite-there responses in our marking. If we solely rely on short, prepared models that are not representative of the final desired outcome, we are not giving a clear example of fully written articulation. How often have we flicked through a student's book, shocked at minimal output in volume or quality? But to defend the student, how many times have they witnessed, discussed and dissected content that matches our expectations, but also helps to form those expectations for themselves?

Modelling can also be rendered ineffective if it fails to account for students' prior knowledge or for cognitive load. Even prepared models seeded within units of learning can prove problematic because they do not attend to the needs of the class at that stage of their learning. That is not to say that modelling cannot take such a form, but it is key we consider how we model within the classroom setting, how many different forms this takes, and how responsive it is to the curricular needs of the student.

When modelling for students, we need to offer:

1. Examples of the processes required to reach the final product (*live*)
2. Examples of the final product (*prepared*)
3. A gradual shift between prepared modelled examples and examples written live, with the level of guidance adjusted in response to student need (*faded*)

These must be accompanied with effective narration so that in time, students can produce high-quality work, independent of our instruction. It is also worth noting that when delivering new content, it can be incredibly

---

98. Haston, W. (2007) 'Teacher Modelling as an Effective Teaching Strategy', *Music Educators Journal*, 93 (4), 26–30.

problematic to provide a prepared example to do so; we run the risk of overburdening working memory by asking students to understand the final product without a firm grasp of the processes and key components of knowledge that lead to the completion of said product in the first place.

For instance, if we were to share an exemplar response that explores to what extent Hyde is presented as a dangerous outsider before students have read the entire novella by Stevenson, or been taught the complexities of what it meant to be an outsider within the Victorian era – James Adams' exploration of masculinity, or David Wright's exploration of mental disability through institutionalisation, for example – then what do we hope they gain from studying the example? This will typically result in cognitive overload, as students grapple with both the knowledge and the process of writing a response using the knowledge. If we do not take account of cognitive load when modelling, we risk exerting working memory beyond its capacity, resulting in students being unable to meet the demands of the task.[99] Simply put, we cannot teach a significant body of new knowledge and teach how to apply that knowledge at the same time.

Live modelling

Live modelling is vital for students to gain a keen understanding of thinking and procedures in action so they may apply these to their own work. However, the cognitive load generated by this process needs to be tempered through a secure knowledge of the content and ideally of the procedure itself to avoid overburdening working memory. If we are modelling text annotation, the text should have already been explored so that students are familiar with the content, ensuring the focus is on the process and not on initial comprehension. Similarly, if we model the dissection of a heart, students should be able to not only identify the pulmonary trunk, aorta and superior vena cava, but also to navigate the coronary sinus to identify the front of the heart, in order for them to confidently follow the dissection process. To ensure that live modelling

---

99. De Jong, T. (2010) 'Cognitive Load Theory, educational research, and instructional design: Some food for thought', *Instructional Science*, 38 (2): 105–134.

places emphasis upon the process, we must consider what core knowledge has preceded it, so that new material does not pose as a distraction.

This metacognitive approach models how to apply knowledge and not just acquire it. Students should gain an insight into the enactment of your subject through the process of watching an expert demonstrate it. The modelling process also draws students' attention to the relationship between the different components they have learnt and how these are successfully drawn together. For instance, if we want to exemplify the process of product design, we might share the process of sketching before we fine-line and then render, to understand how each stage of this process is instrumental to the production itself.

Live modelling allows students to witness these threads being weaved together, with attention paid to the patterns that emerge from this modelling in action. Once these patterns have been shared, discussed and reviewed, students can then experiment using the same patterns in their own responses, with a keen focus on the act of crafting through this shared process. Whilst success criteria may bullet point what needs to be included in a response, these can seem highly abstract to students, whereas live models demonstrate what these standards look like in concrete terms and the process required to create them, subsequently developing students' assessment literacy.[100]

Live modelling is challenging because it pulls from our own cognitive reserves to demonstrate and articulate sometimes complex procedures, whilst drawing attention to and counteracting any possible pitfalls along the way. The challenges encountered in explaining thinking in action can be addressed through precision and practice. Many teachers find live modelling problematic and report that they make mistakes during the process, but this in itself can be conducive to countering the myth that a piece of work is instantly perfect. There are also several practical methods that may help develop our proficiency in live modelling: pre-recording

100. Price, M. et al. (2012) *Assessment Literacy: The Foundation for Improving Student Learning*. Wheatley: Oxford Brookes University.

ourselves, observing others, or preparing brief notes to act as a micro-script all develop our expertise in what is an invaluable way to enact our subject within the classroom.

- How will modelling demonstrate both the thinking and procedure required to complete this task?
- What knowledge do your students possess to safeguard them from cognitive overload?
- How do you prepare to demonstrate this process as the subject expert?

Prepared modelling

Prepared exemplars are an ideal way to demonstrate the end product for students alongside the process; students cannot be expected to apply knowledge without a clear indication of what the gold standard of doing so would resemble. It is also important to consider the standard of the modelled piece at different stages of the curriculum. In Toa and Carless' study of this, one student noted 'being able to identify the weaknesses and improve them are two different things. We knew the problems, but we had no idea how to improve the quality. Rewriting the weak sample makes me realise my own problems when writing the essay.'[101] Weak examples enable students to identify them as weak, but do not always move students forward to being able to see how to correct errors in the example, or in their own work. Once again, we would need to revert to the live model to help them with this.

Exemplars prepared in advance are effective if accompanied by an outline of where the exemplar meets a high standard. In effect, the exemplar is only as effective as the way in which it is used. Nevertheless, we sometimes rely on clumsy formula to achieve this and produce a pale substitute of success as a result. 'Success criteria' that asks students to identify the components of a response before they can really grasp the literacy, mechanisms or purpose of what a truly successful response looks like, are unlikely to

---

101. Toa, J. & Carless, D. (2014) 'Making productive use of exemplars: Peer discussion and teacher guidance for positive transfer of strategies', *Journal of Further and Higher Education*, 40 (6), 746–764.

take students much beyond mimicry. Simply stated, showing the final product against a mark scheme is insufficient for students to understand the journey to the final product: they must have an expert to guide them through each stage of the process.

Whether it is studying exemplar hypothetical testing conclusions, or demonstrating the way in which Johnstone's triangle has been used to outline macroscopic, symbolic and sub-microscopic representations, the prepared example should not act as an oracle-like instrument for how it must be done, whilst the student watches on with the intention to mimic what is presented. Alternatively, by accompanying the dissection of the model with questions which nudge students further in their own interpretation, we enable students to join the teacher in this dissection, so they can apply the process of reassembly for themselves. This becomes incredibly powerful as students begin to actualise both the construction and reconfiguration of the final product. As we will visit during our examination of backwards faded instruction, the enquiry that we choose to employ alongside exemplars decides what students will learn from the exemplar themselves. Ask why the use of the verb, 'proud' to describe the lark within McGowan's depiction within the book of the same title, and students will focus upon the narrator's interpretation of the bird which could then lead into a discussion of how his depiction reflects his situation at that moment. Ask why the writer juxtaposes the word 'proud' alongside 'blood-red' to depict the recently deceased bird's eye, and this will guide students into an insight of the animalistic defiance of death at the hands of mankind. The question leads the discussion, and the teacher must choose which path will be of most value to students at both that point, in the context of prior knowledge, with a view to where learning will lead to next.

- Use prepared modelling to demonstrate the final product.
- Provide high-quality examples of what a gold standard looks like – then break this down into its granular components.
- Demand an active participant when using prepared modelling.

Backwards faded instruction

Backwards fading (using a phased modelling process of I, we, you) is a hybrid of both live and prepared modelling. This process requires a 'fading' of support from the teacher, from high-level instruction and support, through stages of collaboration, to independent practice – continually moving back and forth between each stage depending on the complexity and cognitive effort of the task.

In a Maths lesson for example, the teacher may model solving an equation, narrating the process and drawing attention to possible misconceptions at each stage. Students then solve a similar equation, explaining to the teacher at each stage of the process any issues they have to collectively work through the problem. Students then have a third equation to solve, using mini whiteboards and being given time to complete the new equation on their own before holding up their answers at a specified time. The teacher can make a quick check for correct completion; those with correct answers can move on to completing several similar equations that may incrementally increase in difficulty (but not so much as to go beyond deliberate practise of the question style at hand). The teacher then remains with those who answered incorrectly, working through misconceptions and practising together, repeating the process until all students can confidently move to independent practice.

The teacher may also move forward and backward throughout these stages within a lesson, continuously checking students' proficiency and understanding as a guide for which stage to pause at or move on from.

Faded modelling can also offer an effective mechanism to teach new content, alternating between the 'I' and 'we' stages of the process, removing support gradually until students are confident and informed enough with the knowledge required to apply it independently of support. Essentially, 'I, we, you' takes the form of, 'I, we, I, we, I, we, you, we, you'. This does not mean that the problem itself will always have students complete the last part or first part independently, collectively, or with the teacher – levels of support may vary both within and between tasks. The teacher may model how to write an introduction then the class may collectively write an alternative introduction for the same essay question or for a different one. Alternatively, the class may collaboratively write the next paragraph of the essay, then write the third paragraph independently.

We can take an even more granular approach than this, employing sentence-level modelling with the teacher modelling effective sentence construction, followed by students completing a second using a sentence stem, before writing their own sentence independently. We can also work backwards and forwards in the stages of the task itself by asking students to answer the first stage of an equation before the teacher models its completion, and then working in the opposite direction with the teacher answering the first stage of the equation and then students completing the rest. The versatility of this method contributes to its effectiveness as it allows the teacher to be entirely responsive to both student and task.

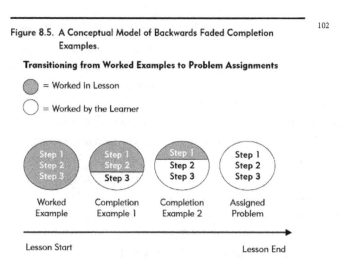

Figure 8.5. A Conceptual Model of Backwards Faded Completion Examples.[102]

Transitioning from Worked Examples to Problem Assignments

⬤ = Worked in Lesson

◯ = Worked by the Learner

| Worked Example | Completion Example 1 | Completion Example 2 | Assigned Problem |

Lesson Start — Lesson End

Transitioning from worked examples to problem assignments with backwards faded modelling

---

102. Clark, R., Nguyen, F. & Sweller, J. (2001) *Efficiency in Learning: Evidence-Based Guidelines to Manage Cognitive Load.* John Wiley & Sons.

Whilst this form of modelling can be used at the micro level of the task itself or its component parts, it may also guide how we use modelling with students across an entire unit. The teacher should look to alternate between 'I' and 'we' interchangeably, until students have secure examples and have fully practised the process before they complete the task independently. At times, we are in danger of rushing through this process when the 'I' and 'we' stages, before independent work, are paramount to student success. Like any form of scaffold, we need to remove these with caution, looking to assure mastery before independence.

Finally, we should take time to evaluate the efficacy of our own instruction and the extent that it is necessary. Silence can be incredibly powerful for the 'I' stage of modelling; Linsin proposes that silence 'purifies your instruction' and rather than reducing support for students, watching without narration for short interludes can improve the presentation of the processes.[103]

With any modelling process, the key finding that arises from research is the teacher's dual role during the process. The teacher imparts the key mechanisms, patterns and procedures of the subject, but in such a way that it encourages student interpretation and not imitation. This layered approach can be achieved through dialogue and a proactive-reactive approach to checking student understanding: *'this process carries out this function. Why is that significant? Why do we need this process at this point? What would be most suitable to follow after it?'* The teacher alternates between the imperative and inquisitive; students are guided seamlessly to and from contemplation, drawing upon prior knowledge back to enquiry, provided with instruction where necessary.

Modelling is such a valuable tool that we should look to embed it at an early point within our established habits of the classroom. 'Front loading' examples of modelling by exposing students to repeated, frequent episodes of modelling at the start of the academic year, which will lead to

---

103. https://www.smartclassroommanagement.com/2014/09/27/why-silent-modeling-is-a-powerful-strategy/

an improved and secure understanding of what it is that you want students to gain from the process, is far more effective than models introduced just before or after an assessment. This should be a key consideration when considering the journey of curriculum; marking out the inclusion of modelling and plotting at earlier points where it will be a necessity means that as these scaffolds are gradually removed, we can be more and more certain that students have been exposed to effective demonstrations of what a high standard looks like within the discipline.

- Do the modelled responses within the classroom act to provide a replication of the outcome or a replication of the process?
- How has the standard of models been quality assured?
- Before they attempt a task independently, how frequently have students seen both the process in action and the final result?

CHAPTER 11
THE POWER OF QUESTIONING

According to Chouinard et al, young children ask between four hundred and twelve hundred questions each week.[104] However, this tapers off as children start school: as we get older, we ask fewer questions.[105, 106] This happens because the environment does not always encourage students to do so. Poor proxies for learning and the way lessons have sometimes reverted to spectacle for graded observations can mean the way we use questions has not always lent itself to effective curriculum delivery. Instead of directing, we have facilitated; instead of asking those who do not know, we asked those who did. Instead of utilising questions as a method of direction through our subject, we used them as a method of exposition without understanding; a way to plough through lessons with the minority that could respond accurately to the question.

Done well, questions are essential to articulate what is known, and what needs to be known to move forward. To ask questions as the teacher means that you have a constant measuring stick of what has been said, how it has been interpreted, and where you might want to go from there. For the student, the more we learn, the more we realise what we do not know, and questions allow students to repeatedly put themselves in a position of low-stakes vulnerability to clarify if what they know to

104. Chouinard, M., Harris, P., & Maratsos, M. (2007) 'Children's Questions: A Mechanism for Cognitive Development', *Monographs of the Society for Research in Child Development*, 72 (1).
105. Dillon, J. T. (1988) 'The remedial status of student questioning', *Journal of Curriculum Studies*, 20 (3), 197–210.
106. Van der Meij, H. (1988) 'Constraints on question asking in classrooms', *Journal of Educational Psychology*, 80 (3), 401–405.

be true is true, but also to continue on the path of establishing what it is that is still unknown. Questions allow students to feel empowered by this vulnerability, positively reinforcing the value of knowledge and more importantly, identifying that further knowledge is of value.

Curating key moment questions

Constructing highly effective questions is one of the most challenging aspects of being a teacher and this process should take precedence in planning a lesson. Deciding which questions will be pertinent at each stage of a lesson, who you may ask them to, how they will be constructed, and how you can ensure that any follow-up questions will assist students in exemplifying, extending or reshaping their answers, should be the foundation of our planning. If we consider the main teaching points in our lesson, and shape our questions around these, we are also more likely to structure our lessons in such a way that students are able to access and respond to what we want them to learn, than if our lessons are driven by activities and tasks. In addition, planning the questions that you will ask both aids the mental rehearsal of a lesson and builds your sense of self-affirmation: the less you have to plan questions for your teaching, the more confident you are in your approach as a practitioner. Developing this aspect of your practice and giving it priority will reap rewards for planning workload.

To plan questions also ensures that we do not overlook what Guy Claxton refers to as 'radiator children': those students that can become passengers in a lesson, not disrupting but not engaging.[107] If we are to ensure our curriculum is enacted in such a way that we can see its impact in the classroom, we need to ensure that our questions are designed to direct learning, identify learning needs, and put us in the best possible position to respond to these needs as effectively as possible.

---

107. Wiliam, D. (2016) 'Assessment for Learning: why, what and how', Institute of Education, University of London, accessed at https://www.dylanwiliam.org/Dylan_Wiliams_website/Papers_files/Cambridge%20 AfL%20keynote.doc.

- How are questions planned and designed to ensure they have a diagnostic quality for all students?

Active anticipation to be chosen

Everyone in the room should feel prepared to participate. We should not offer opting out as an option: not knowing is ok, but the effort to answer should be an expectation, and the effort to hazard an idea should be valued and encouraged. Share with students that you will be asking a question and be explicit in your expectation of a fully rounded response. If there is a lack of response, students should know that you value their ideas and participation enough that you will always return to them for an answer. Change or reshape the question if it helps, or give them the entire lesson to think on a response before they provide one. But always set the expectation that any student may be called upon to answer a question and that you care too much to have them leave the lesson without feeling success and value in their contribution. This ensures a balance between inviting students to feel welcomed to join the discussion, and yet implicitly not providing a way to opt out of it.

The purpose of questions is pivotal to curricular thought, because all students are involved in the discussion. What is important is that students are drawn into the conversation, as opposed to leapt upon to answer. The language used should invite students to consider, share and to participate in a dialogue:

> *Tell me about...*
> *What did you think about...*
> *How do you interpret that?*
> *How might we make sense of that?*

If we want to encourage students to consume critically, we must conduct dialogue in a way that demonstrates the value of their ideas, rather than simply seeking answers so that we can drive onwards through the content.

A note on silence here: 'negative associations with silence may derive from the teacher's personal apprehensions or from their perceptions of what a teacher's role should be.'[108] Although this may seem counterintuitive, silence is vital to our role as teachers; it enhances, rather than takes away. Silence allows thinking to take place, without hindrance or distraction. However, silence can do far more than this:

> Silence can punctuate what has been said, allow us space to absorb it, and allow us to move beyond it. Silence can welcome the silenced to speak. Silence can help us realise the limits and proper uses of language. Silence can cut through the constructs that we are fed and that we feed ourselves.[109]

It is the lack of words that can draw attention to those that preceded it before, and silence is a vital and effective tool for our teaching. At times when silence can seem a deadweight for learning, we would do well to recognise that it acts to provide time to learn, but it must be used with purpose to ensure this level of value. Students might be given silence to consider their prior knowledge within the context of a new scenario – such as their understanding of erosion as a coastal process, after a series of episodes considering erosion as a process of riversides; or when students are completing independent formulae after a series of episodes where the sine or cosine rule has been exemplified through variations of modelled practice. Silence is not a luxury to the classroom, but a necessary component for learning to take place.

- Questions should use language that invites students to answer and makes explicit the value of their contribution.
- Time needs to be built into our curriculum for silence and thinking hard.
- Silence can be a powerful tool for helping students to conceptualise the curriculum.

---

108. Ollin, R. (2008) 'Silent pedagogy and rethinking classroom practice: structuring teaching through silence rather than talk', *Cambridge Journal of Education*, 38 (2), 265–280.
109. Sherrington, T. (2017) *The Learning Rainforest: Great Teaching in Real Classrooms*. John Catt.

Exposing students' thinking

If we want students to think hard, we need to give them the time and space to do so. We need to help students articulate their thinking process so we can explore their answers and the metacognitive processes that got them there, whilst drawing out any misconceptions. When posing a question to the room, take a few moments to pause, with the expectation that everyone has time to mentally prepare, before calling on a student to answer. Names should always be used at the end of our questions, never at the start, so there is a clear expectation for all students to participate. We should also narrate the value of this thinking time to students, explaining that being first to answer is not the goal, but answering thoughtfully is.

Our question should also not necessarily end with a student's answer; we should look to ask the student or others to elaborate, challenge or agree with the response, justifying and developing their ideas. Crucially, this can open up gaps in knowledge itself or in the process students have gone through to find their answer. If we ask students how they know this, or why, rather than accept their first answer, we can tease out misconceptions not just of the original student but also those we ask to take the response further. Simply asking *'how do you know?'* or *'why do you think that?'* can expose the gaps we would not see from the answer alone. Questions should therefore act as a clarification of learning as much as an exploration; it becomes a diagnostic process where the teacher can work meticulously to ascertain what is known, and by whom.

We also need to be mindful that the answers of a handful of students are not indicative of the understanding of the whole class. One student providing the correct answer does not confirm the entire class has understood what has been asked – one person has, and everyone else heard them share it, but we cannot accurately draw conclusions much further than this. This is why our questioning, over time, needs to be iterative and probing, nudging learning forward along the way.

- How does the way in which you pose a question ensure adequate time for mental rehearsal and expose the processes of students' thinking?

Hinge questions provide curricular signposts

Hinge questions offer a powerful diagnostic tool for identifying what students know and can do at key points in the curriculum. They can be used to ensure we gain an accurate snapshot of students' understanding. Hinge questions should take 30 seconds – they should be a short task, not requiring thinking time or time to verbally rehearse and give a response. They should not be onerous on workload or planning, but most importantly, they should be difficult, and impossible to get right for the wrong reason: it should be almost impossible to succeed as a result of guesswork on the student's part.

An effective form for hinge questions are multiple-choice questions with plausible but incorrect distractors[110] whereby through their design we can easily spot the errors in learning. The effectiveness of their design is in the distractors that require secure knowledge to discern them from the correct answers. It can also be valuable to have multiple possible answers in one question but not indicate how many correct answers there are, significantly increasing the room for error and thus making it far easier for the teacher to identify where misconceptions lie.

Here is an example hinge question, outlined by Dylan Wiliam:

The ball sitting on the table is not moving. It is not moving because:

1. *no forces are pushing or pulling on the ball.*
2. *gravity is pulling down, but the table is in the way.*
3. *the table pushes up with the same force that gravity pulls down.*
4. *gravity is holding it onto the table.*
5. *there is a force inside the ball keeping it from rolling off the table.*

In this question, the student meets several possible pitfalls:

---

110. Wiliam, D. (2015) 'Designing Great Hinge Questions', *Questioning for Learning*, 73 (1), 40–44.

- They may not understand the role of force.
- They may not understand the role of gravity in accordance with Newton's law of motion.
- They may not understand the role that force has at rest.
- They may not understand the relationship that force has with gravity.

All four incorrect options are plausible; all are common errors. A. signposts a lack of understanding in force; B. demonstrates understanding to an extent; D. highlights gaps in knowledge around the way in which gravity can operate; E. provides a more significant concern in the way not only the student has failed to grasp force and gravity, but also around the introductory study of atomic structure at KS3. Using hinge questions in this way allows the teacher to quickly identify where students may fall short and look to rectify this. Acting as a tool to direct what and how content is taught next, this forensic approach helps us to make informed decisions about the next steps for our students. No lollipop sticks, no guesswork – just solid, incisive measurement of whether to move forward and how to do so.

- How and where can hinge questions identify misconceptions and signpost students' current level of understanding?

CHAPTER 12
THE LANGUAGE
OF OUR SUBJECTS

Before we move into a consideration of how to support teachers in curriculum enactment, we must take the time to explore how oracy fits within the representation of our subjects, both of the verbal and written variety. To ensure that the curriculum is conveyed in a way that is truthful and faithful to the nuances of the discipline itself, we must consider how we speak of and about it.

Oracy and the curriculum

Student and teacher oracy is our curriculum in action; to articulate, understand and contemplate the subject, we must be able to speak it. Students must hear us model the way to correctly and respectfully address the language of our subject if we expect them to do so in turn. The national curriculum seeks to streamline the inclusion of spoken language in such a manner that it is arguably no longer fit for purpose; the primary framework stipulates that spoken language underpins reading, but beyond the requirement for children to be able to speak in-role, requires little in terms of a robust approach,[111] and the GCSE specification for English language no longer recognises speaking and listening as a formal component of the overall grade. However, cognitive science and ongoing research recognises the intrinsic relationship between learning and articulation of learning: the cognitive gains made through maintaining a high standard of oracy in

---

111. https://assets.publishing.service.gov.uk/government/uploads/system/uploads/attachment_data/file/335186/PRIMARY_national_curriculum_-_English_220714.pdf

the classroom are undeniable in their role in articulating understanding and contributing to students' retention of subject-specific knowledge.[112]

Whilst didactic, explicit teaching is essential for imparting knowledge, this return to a teacher-led classroom has in some cases misconstrued and diminished the need for students to be provided with the time and models to convey their ideas in a way that not only ensures they engage with the curriculum, but that they can contemplate complex concepts for themselves. This is simply not possible if we speak and they do not. Equally, the definition of an oracy education has been somewhat misdefined and misinterpreted as relying on dialogic teaching – what we may refer to as 'discovery learning' through group-led discussion. This has led to the false dichotomy in some interpretations that either we let students speak and they find their own path to knowledge, or we speak and instruct the path for them. Mercer differentiates between the two succinctly here:

> Oracy education is the direct, explicit teaching of speaking and listening skills as part of the language and literacy curriculum, comparable to the direct, explicit teaching of algebra as part of maths. Dialogic teaching is a set of talk-based strategies for teaching any subject, whether it be maths, history, English or whatever.[113]

For the purpose of clarity, it is an oracy education that we seek to achieve through teacher exemplar and student rehearsal; not unaided and unsupported student discussion where the practice and development of sophisticated oracy is left to chance.

Preferably, our delivery of the curriculum has anticipated where students require time to shape their ideas. We provide suitable and manageable models of how our subject is discussed and demonstrated; teachers use terminology within

---

112. Jay, T., Willis, B., Thomas, P. et al. (2017) *Dialogic Teaching: Evaluation report and executive summary.* Education Endowment Foundation.
113. Mercer, N. (2018) 'Oracy education and dialogic teaching: what's the difference?' Oracy Cambridge. Accessed at https://oracycambridge.org/2018/02/22/oracy-education-and-dialogic-teaching-whats-the-difference/.

the framework of a discussion, which in turn becomes second nature to the students as they are provided with the opportunity to handle such terminology for themselves. WWI is the First World War; equipment becomes apparatus; germs become pathogens; the width of a circle becomes the diameter. Such micro-changes might seem insignificant, but they not only elevate the subject, imbuing a sense of reverence and respect to the discipline, but this repeated rehearsal also enables students to actualise the subject for themselves.

Vocabulary to unlock our subjects

Within our teaching of oracy, and in all the ways we articulate our discipline and ask students to do the same, there comes the need to explicitly teach and model vocabulary that takes students beyond everyday discourse and begins to unlock our subjects. Vocabulary instruction can be one of the most powerful ways to close the gap for our students and helps them to master deep subject knowledge. For vocabulary to be taught effectively, we need to explicitly teach:

- morphology – prefixes and suffixes and the way words are formed
- etymology – word origins (a discrete element of morphology)
- vocabulary in context – how words work in a sentence.

Paying attention to morphology can unlock students' understanding of thousands of words as '90% of English words of two or more syllables have Latin and Greek roots'.[114] Knowing the prefix *mal* originates from the Latin for 'bad' or 'evil' can help students to understand words such as 'malevolent', 'malicious' or 'malignant'. In science, knowing that 'menses' originates from the Latin *mensis* or 'month' can help unlock students' understanding of menstruation occurring monthly (give or take) or menopause being a 'pause' in the monthly cycle. When students make connections between words and their roots, they are forming stronger schematic webs by adding another layer to their understanding.

For vocabulary instruction to be effective, it needs to be applied in both spoken and written models. When introducing new vocabulary, teachers

---

114. Myatt, M. (2018) *The Curriculum: Gallimaufry to Coherence.* John Catt.

should use the word in the context of at least three sentences, either written or spoken, and use synonyms to support understanding. We should also insist that written work includes key vocabulary that is used and spelled accurately. Lists of key vocabulary alongside sentence exemplars are useful as a scaffold, but we also need to ensure that these words are understood within their contexts. Presenting examples of the word used in different sentences, both in everyday conversation and in the context of the text or topic being studied, is an effective way to model this as it demonstrates how the word applies to the lesson as well as its wider, everyday contexts.

We can go even further in ensuring students have a secure understanding of new vocabulary through carefully structured application tasks. It is not enough to ask students to simply use the word in their own sentences as this does not always highlight misconceptions. To avoid these, asking students to use the new vocabulary in their own sentence but to include the word *because* can help ensure they have a secure understanding. If a student writes 'The subjects were submissive to the queen', we cannot necessarily be sure they know what the word 'submissive' means – we can assume, but it is worth pushing for more. If we ask students to continue the sentence with 'because' to explain the context of the word, we can be much more confident that they understand this vocabulary in context ('The subjects were submissive to the queen because they immediately obeyed her orders'). If a student were to write 'The subjects were submissive to the queen because they gave her orders', we know something has gone wrong. With a quick check over shoulders and a few sentences shared, we can quickly establish whether students have a good understanding or if a little more explanation and modelling is required. Being deliberate in our teaching of vocabulary helps induct students into the rich language of our subject and gives them a language to articulate it in.

- Frequent exposure to high-quality oracy is essential to effective curriculum enactment.
- Explicit instruction and modelling of oracy and vocabulary can unlock our subjects for students, offering the language and means to articulate it for themselves.

SECTION FOUR: A FRAMEWORK FOR DEVELOPMENT
CULTIVATION OF THE CURRICULUM

The development, review and refinement of the curriculum will only be successful if it is a collective pursuit. This is only possible with the requisite culture and systems in place to support it. We need an institutional agreement that curriculum will take priority, with well-governed systems that improve and refine such work on a continual and dedicated loop of review with a clear commitment to frequent and purposeful dialogue. This section explores how such systems can be designed and implemented to ensure that the ongoing development of our curriculum and our teachers, is effective, meaningful and conducive to continual improvement.

CHAPTER 13
PEOPLE DEVELOPMENT IS
CURRICULAR DEVELOPMENT

Curriculum work demands a systematic approach to professional development that drives and motivates teachers to become experts in their subjects and in their classroom practice. It is too simplistic and naive for us to believe that putting people to work on curriculum means curriculum work will be successful. We need to understand and harness the working dynamics of our teams to bring our combined curriculum thinking into fruition. The complexity of curriculum work invites challenge and we need to create a collegiate space for this challenge to take place. Mary Myatt highlights the need to nurture this collegiality in *High Challenge, Low Threat*:

> Sensible leaders understand the quiet importance of the relationship, they pay attention to it and cultivate it. Essentially they honour the relationship because people enjoy doing business with people they like. It's as simple as that.[115]

It is not enough for us to know what needs to be undertaken; we need to understand the people who will undertake it – how they are motivated, how they operate, and how this should be cultivated. Work on the curriculum is where the teacher can fully utilise their expertise with a deep sense of satisfaction for the job as a whole; it is vital that we offer teachers such an experience.

---

115.   Myatt, M. (2016) *High Challenge, Low Threat*. John Catt Educational Limited, 2016.

To improve curricular engagement, we would do well to look at our models of professional practice. We need to ensure meetings focus on professional development, not administration; that pedagogy is contextual and supports the needs of the teacher; that performance systems look to develop the teacher in action; and that data outcomes over which teachers have very little influence are not used as a measure of teacher quality.[116] To develop and empower the profession and to achieve the curriculum quality we strive towards, we need new models for how we train and develop teachers.

It is all too simplistic to assume that accountability is the opposite of trust. When trust and accountability are combined and well-employed, they are arguably the most effective tools we have to support work as complex as curriculum development. In practice, this combination of accountability and trust manifests itself in a senior leader's probing inquiry to ascertain the current contentions of a subject, whilst trusting the subject lead's expertise and insights to guide them. A subject lead will focus the team's efforts to establish where there are compromised areas of curriculum, employing transparent, forensic inquiry, and looking to support and find solutions that bring the team together, in a way that goes beyond the surface analysis of the last set of assessment results.

Methods of accountability, when executed effectively, can be a healthy process of review and improvement. However, we know that accountability can take a different form and can sometimes feel intrusive, threaten to sidetrack us or be counterproductive. The key to accountability is in its moderation: too little, or what the NFER accountability review refers to as 'lighter touch,'[117] and we potentially undermine the value and worth of the work taking place; adopt a more rigid, hierarchical approach, and we risk overlooking the nuances of the discipline as we construct a one-size-fits-all approach. Vanhoof and Petegem look to identify the role of accountability and how this can inform our approach:

---

116. Shakeshaft, N. G., Trzaskowski, M., McMillan, A., Rimfeld, K., Krapohl, E. et al. (2013) 'Strong Genetic Influence on a UK Nationwide Test of Educational Achievement at the End of Compulsory Education at Age 16', *PLOS One*, 8 (12), https://doi.org/10.1371/journal.pone.0080341.

117. Brill, F., Grayson, H. & Kuhn, L. (2018) *What Impact Does Accountability Have On Curriculum, Standards and Engagement In Education? A Literature Review.* Slough: NFER.

The distinction between the two perspectives (accountability and school improvement) is based on different answers to the questions of (1) whether quality assurance is primarily concerned with monitoring and accountability or rather with development and improvement and (2) to the question of who determines 'quality of education', in other words: the government or the school itself.[118]

When we design policy and procedure that supports teacher and curriculum development, a focus on student outcomes will unlikely be conducive to this aim. Measuring student performance as a proxy for the quality of teaching will not improve its quality. This leaves us with the question: how do we work to improve teaching of the curriculum? Where do we focus our attention in developing expert teachers if student outcomes do not act as an accurate measure?

James Clear, author of *Atomic Habits*, outlines a key principle which may be applicable here:

True long-term thinking is goalless thinking. It's not about any single accomplishment. It is about the cycle of endless refinement and continuous improvement. Ultimately, it is your commitment to the process that will determine your progress.[119]

Therefore, to develop teachers, and improve the outcomes that will likely follow, focus needs to be on the process of improvement and the ongoing endeavours that will encourage it. We should distance ourselves from distractions of data analysis and exam grades as indicative of effective curriculum development, and look to improve our work through a focus on developing professional expertise in the form of high-quality training, evaluation, reflection and conversation.

118. Vanhoof, J. & Van Petegem, P. (2007) 'Matching internal and external evaluation in an era of accountability and school development: Lessons from a Flemish perspective', *Studies in Educational Evaluation*, 33, 101–119.
119. Clear, J. (2018) *Atomic Habits*. New York: Avery.

- Accountability and trust are not diametrically opposed.
- Accountability should act to promote professional development.
- Student performance in examinations is an inaccurate measure of curriculum and teacher quality.
- Focusing on teacher development is more likely to improve student outcomes than if these are used as an accountability measure.

Identification of need

Curriculum review is change management in action; whilst other sectors might review staffing structures or policy, our process involves the work of the curriculum. Consequently, this continual loop of review means that we need an ethos and culture to match.

Trust is essential to change. Professor Vivianne Robinson outlines three key capabilities that are necessary to successfully managing change within schools:

1. *Using relevant knowledge from research and experience.*
2. *Using this knowledge to solve the complex educational problems that stand in the way of achieving improvement goals.*
3. *Building relationships of trust with those involved.*[120]

We should not look to remedy what might not be broken. Equally, we cannot attempt to solve a problem unless all collective parties recognise it as such. Robinson proposes taking an objective, evidence-informed approach to identifying the problem, sharing this with the team, then working together towards pragmatic solutions:

> Leaders cannot solve such problems on their own. They need to build trust with teachers who may be sceptical; who have different beliefs about what works in their classrooms; and who may be

---

120. Robinson, V. M. J. (2019) 'Excellence in educational leadership: Practices, capabilities and virtues that foster improved student outcomes', in T. Bush, L. Bell & D. Middlewood (eds.), *Principles of Educational Leadership and Management.* Sage Publications.

tired of change. In education, problem-solving is a largely social process, and it requires leaders at all levels to have high ability in the third capability, that of building relational trust.

The social aspect of problem-solving relies heavily on the trust and mutual respect that we afford to all who contribute. Building trust is more than simply handing over the reins; it is being deliberate in establishing a sense of collegiality between those undertaking the work and those overseeing and supporting it.

- Undertake change management through accurate identification of the issue.
- Seek active alignment with the rationale for change, rather than compliance.
- Value trust and the collective pursuit of resolution.

Agreed standards

We cannot impart a collection of principles for curricular development without the right drivers and voices to guide it. Dialogue to drive curriculum has never been more vital; as Susan Scott outlines, 'the conversation is the relationship.'[121] We build trust through our collective sense of purpose as we work collaboratively to unpick, evaluate and refine. All members carry out a role that feels useful and effective, allowing autonomy but from a common starting place agreed through our collective conversations.

Once we undertake the initial work of establishing our common goal, we need to communicate and establish the standard of quality – what we are working towards, and what it might resemble. If leading such work, particularly where there will be contentions around how it should look or the choices we should make, it becomes all the more imperative that these standards are outlined beforehand and a consensus is found. If the system of quality assurance and model of success are collectively agreed, they are far more likely to be met.

---

121. Scott, S. (2002) *Fierce conversations: achieving success at work & in life, one conversation at a time.* New York: Viking.

We can sometimes assume that a curriculum map, handbook or vision statement offers sufficient guidance in supporting our teams. However, for our curriculum work to be successful, we need to be explicit in forming an agreed standard for what this will look like in practice. This may involve agreeing key foci for development for the year, such as the regular use of high-quality models, or a deliberate focus on the teaching of vocabulary, or employing common language and micro-scripts, all guided by an agreed standard of quality in the classroom. Whatever the chosen focus may be, this must be explained, modelled, and given the time and status it deserves, as opposed to existing only on a document.

- Establish the standards for your subject team– where do we excel in (insert subject)?
- How do we know? What does this look like in practice?

Respectful honesty

Valuing honesty in our everyday work leads to effective communication and clarification of what high standards look like. If we look to discuss curricular work candidly, but temper this with a respect for teachers as experts in their own right, this will drive successful curriculum conversation.

Conversations that employ a concise, transparent approach are welcomed far more than we might think, and when they are coupled with kindness, the work becomes a joy. Kim Scott outlines such an approach succinctly here:

> Often when people give feedback, they're not as clear or helpful as they might think… being professional too often [means] this gets translated as, 'leave your humanity, the very best part of yourself, at home'.[122]

Honesty can sometimes be misconstrued as unkindness, but failing to provide honest feedback can be unkindness in itself, because we are doing a disservice to those who deserve feedback the most. This 'ruinous

---

122. Scott. K (2017), *Radical Candor*. MacMillan.

empathy'[123] can be deeply damaging to a team: a group of people who find it impossible to be honest with each other simply cannot create work of a high quality. Praise without focus, quickly returned and devoid of specifics, gives fleeting attention to what matters, leaving people uncertain of what high-quality work looks like. When we give feedback that looks to flatter rather than to support, it renders that feedback empty. Scott outlines:

> We're conditioned from an early age to avoid hurting people's feelings. It's not a bad impulse to protect people's feelings, but it's a short-lived protection. You need to rise above your empathy and realize that it's your own feelings you are protecting, not theirs.

It is a disservice to members of your team to provide feedback that offers any less than a sense of continual improvement and a model for their feedback to others. Teams who acknowledge that the focus is to improve the work, and that this is only possible through continual refinement, quickly learn to put aside ego or insecurity and recognise the adaptations as opportunities to improve not only the curriculum, but their capacity to understand it. Creating a culture of honest feedback with a focus on continual improvement and a clear framework to support it can make this process of collaboration one of the most satisfying aspects of our roles in schools.

Creating opportunities for feedback that are less formal, which expose others to well-curated work without it being formally presented as such, allows for a light-touch approach to continual feedback. For example, a centrally shared document or resource where teachers can make suggestions that focus on the work, tweaking and adjusting it with small conversations to refine or modify, creates opportunity for subtle honesty from all. To create a culture of genuine collaboration, we must create the conditions to be critically honest. Communicating that the curriculum does not belong to any one person, but is the collective responsibility of us all, is an ideal starting point to achieve this.

---

123. Ibid.

- Value honesty and temper it with kindness.
- View accountability as an integral part of curriculum conversations.
- Offer ongoing opportunities for feedback.

Collegiately over compliance

If we are to move to a culture where collaboration is a natural and necessary conductor of curriculum, it must be the right type of collaboration, where those who work on the curriculum act as a collegiate instead of simply yielding to the work. Judith Little outlines this succinctly:

> Collaborations may arise naturally out of the problems and circumstances that teachers experience in common, but often they appear contrived, inauthentic, grafted on, perched precariously (and often temporarily) on the margins of real work.[124]

To ensure that curriculum development is meaningful to everyone involved, staff must be included in the process to create a true alignment of purpose rather than simple compliance. The presence of coherent mental models is required for such work to take place so that we can better align our aims and encourage effective professional dialogue.

- We need to build a framework to cultivate teachers' expertise through effective professional development.
- Meaningful discourse is key to effective curriculum review.
- A culture of collaboration and collegiality is vital for curriculum development.

Developing mental models

For our collective purpose and responsibility to be enacted, our conversations around curriculum should be meaningful and not at cross-purposes. We need to offer suitable opportunities to discuss curriculum without obligation or judgement: to talk about the subject for the subject's

---

124. Little, J. W. (1990) 'The Persistence of Privacy: Autonomy and Initiative in Teachers? Professional Relations', *Teachers College Record*, 91.

sake, outside of motive, agenda or accountability. These conversations are central to our work and require skill and an aligned mental model to be effective. The working principle of mental models originally conceptualised by Johnson-Laird is outlined as:

> Knowledge structure(s) held by each member of a team that enables them to form accurate explanations and expectations... and in turn, to coordinate their actions and adapt their behaviour to demands of the task and other team members.[125]

Gentner develops this further to assert that high-quality shared mental models can move us from novice to expert in the art of effective conversation itself. These mental models might exist in the form of quality assurance agreements, or micro-scripts used for teaching particularly complex concepts within the classroom. It may be the use of research papers relevant to the subject which can be used to establish the standards within a subject discipline's delivery. The use of shared mental models – developing common language and undergoing the process of accompanying discussions – enables us to not only identify issues or obstacles collectively, but also use our combined knowledge and experience to consider the most strategically effective way for us to overcome problems.[126] The process itself strengthens our expertise, better equipping us to address similar issues or contentions in the future. As illustrated within the model of siloed views that can exist when a team come together to tackle a specific issue, there are tensions between the individual perspective, the disparity this creates for possibility of a shared perspective, and the issue itself.

125. Fletcher, J. D. & Sottilare, R. A. 'Shared Mental Models in Support of Adaptive Instruction for Teams Using the GIFT Tutoring Architecture', *International Journal of Artificial Intelligence in Education*, 28, 265–285.
126. Gentner, D. & Stevens, A. L. (eds.) (1983) *Mental Models*. Psychology Press.

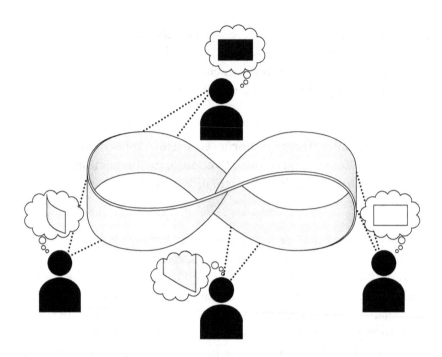

Siloed views – bounded rationality[127]

When a team comes to a problem with differing previous experiences, domain-specific knowledge or external influence over their own perspective and rationale to resolve a problem, this may result in a varying perspective of the problem itself. To eradicate the possibility of each member viewing the issue at hand in an entirely different way, the establishment of common language in advance reduces the probability of not being on the same page, as it were. This preparatory task, coupled with discussions that enable trust and honesty to coexist, lead to professional discourse and action planning that forms a shared mental model instead:

127. Taken from Simple Complexity by William Donaldson, accessed at https://simplecomplexitybook. com/2017/09/10/mental-models-and-the-mobius-strip/.

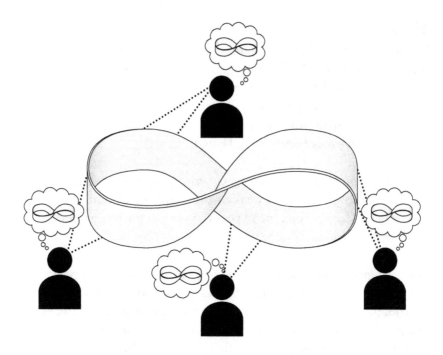

Shared system view – common mental model[128]

Less experienced designers of curriculum need to see repeated instances of coming together to discuss its complexities so they encounter several working examples in how to resolve issues in the future. Conversation as professional development cannot be overlooked.

- Take time to talk about the subject for the subject's sake, outside of motive, agenda or accountability.
- Encourage effective mental models for yourself and your teams by promoting professional conversation.
- Use these conversations to support less experienced teachers in seeing this process of problem-solving in action.

---

128. Ibid.

The absence of an endpoint

The work of the curriculum is never done, and the importance of this is sometimes overlooked. It may mean that we do not gain any tangible sense of completion and the satisfaction that goes with it. We must therefore seek satisfaction through conversations around curriculum, knowing that value is to be sought from the work along the way and not in an endpoint. Our perspective may benefit from being reframed:

> Perfection is never the case when writing curriculum. It doesn't matter how many times we review and edit curriculum work; it is never 'done'... I commend you who venture forth in a quest to create 'thinking cultures'.[129]

Using language that encourages curriculum as ongoing, ever-reviewed, and problematic but enduring, enables a team to not only value their contribution, but also to recognise that professional fulfilment and intrinsic motivation is found in the discussions that sound out curricular development, as opposed to the pretence of a finish line.

- Do your curriculum conversations encourage intrinsic motivation by valuing contributions and recognising the knowledge and expertise of all participants?

---

129. Lanning, L. A. (2012), *Designing a Concept-based Curriculum for English Language Arts.* Corwin Press.

CHAPTER 14
TEACHER DEVELOPMENT IS
CURRICULAR DEVELOPMENT

Supporting and including less experienced or novice teachers in curriculum work is vital to its longevity. If we are to future-proof curriculum quality, we need to ensure that the curriculum designers of the future are fully equipped to design. However, we also need to ensure our training and development of teachers is precise and specific to their needs. For example, Berliner illustrates how feedback to novice teachers often lacks the required focus, foundations and context for it to be useful:

> Novices are taught context-free rules such as 'give praise for right answers', 'wait 3 seconds after asking a higher order question', and 'never personally criticize a student'.[130]

The lack of contextual, domain-specific knowledge in such feedback – with the underlying implication that once these aspects of teaching practice are achieved, mastery will follow – implicitly suggests the endpoint for becoming an expert teacher is in following a formula. We look to quick-fix remedies that are 'easy' to employ at a superficial level, but they fail to improve the teacher in the classroom. Additionally, such measures and guidance may act as temporary remedies for novice teachers, but we cannot hang the process of curriculum enactment on such an inflexible and vague method of feedback which is disconnected from the subject itself.

---

130. Berliner, D. (2004) 'Describing the behavior and documenting the accomplishments of expert teachers', *Bulletin of Science, Technology & Society*, 24 (3), 200–212.

The effectiveness of our questioning, explanations and modelling all hinge on our subject knowledge. More often than not, it is less that a teacher struggles to construct effective question structures but more that they do not have the subject knowledge required to know what those questions should be. Directing a teacher to 'improve their questioning skills' is so vague as to be detrimental to their practice. Simply asking teachers to use 'more open questions' also does not get us very far, particularly when closed questions can be a very effective diagnostic tool. Our focus needs to be on the subject itself and how teaching practice and its improvement can be shaped around it. If we spend more time supporting new teachers in developing their subject knowledge and being precise in how they can use this to inform their questions, models and explanations, we get better teaching practice as a result.

- Feedback on teaching practice needs to be precise and contextual.
- Developing subject knowledge develops teaching practice.

Instructional coaching for curricular improvement

Whilst we focus on developing subject knowledge as a way of developing teacher practice, we can look to where iterative, instructional coaching can support its enactment. Rather than long-form observations which identify multiple areas for improvement that are often far too generic or vague to be of practical use, this form of coaching focuses on pinpointing one specific element of practice to hone and develop over time to ensure that its use becomes habitual in the classroom. It acts as a tool to drive improvement by 'focusing on the one thing'. This 'one thing' is set within the context of the lesson but is actionable for future lessons, allowing teachers to pay close attention to their deliberate actions and language in order to improve their practice via incremental steps. These steps ask teachers to make micro-adjustments to their teaching, drawing attention to their practice as a result.

For example, a novice teacher might be guided by their coach to focus on posing a question and ensuring they call on a student by name at the end of the question and not the beginning, or to script common language they will use for an upcoming explanation or sequence of modelling. These specific, immediately actionable steps may only be relevant for one lesson, but they expose the process of planning or delivery as a result. They are effective in supporting teachers to improve their practice whilst not feeling overwhelming or unmanageable.

Coaching steps that draw attention to both the action and the process also encourage teachers to become more consciously competent in what they do by breaking down their practice into granular steps, making the micro-decisions of teaching more visible, and helping them to be more aware of the effortful nature of their enactment. Through deliberate practice of this step or technique, we begin to move towards unconscious competence whereby this improvement in delivery becomes habitual and no longer requires conscious effort; this is the mark of successful teacher development.

- Move away from long-form observations that identify multiple, often generic areas for improvement.
- Focus on one thing at a time to deliberately rehearse, practise and review.

Culture and mechanisms for instructional coaching

Incremental, instructional coaching requires a culture of continuous improvement in schools, without judgement or hierarchy, with all teachers coached and many as coaches, as a sign of our continual pursuit to get better. The oft-repeated quote from Dylan Wiliam makes clear:

> Every teacher needs to improve, not because they are not good enough, but because they can be even better.[131]

However, we also need the mechanisms to support all teachers in getting better. Well-designed programmes such as Powerful Action Steps[132] are an

---

131. Wiliam, D. (2012) keynote speech at the SSAT Conference in December 2012.
132. Powerful Action Steps is an online platform for instructional coaching designed by Josh Goodrich.

ideal example of how we can systematically employ what we know about the effectiveness of instructional coaching in a way that is accessible and actionable. Through the design of such platforms and the process of using them, not only do we support teachers in becoming better teachers, but also help them become better coaches by offering a framework that guides them in doing so. We thereby improve and empower our teachers in both their own classroom and when supporting others in theirs.

The successful enactment of curriculum requires a responsive, iterative cycle of identification, refinement, and evolution; by placing our focus on developing subject knowledge and the incremental improvements we can make to both its design and delivery, we can hope to be more successful in both.

- All teachers can get better; focus on improvement should not be hierarchical.
- We need mechanisms and systems in place to support the implementation of instruction coaching.

Autonomy and personalised teacher development

Daniel Pink proposes that 'when professionals are told what to do and given no choice, the best possible outcome is likely compliance— and compliance is not enough to do the complex work needed in our schools'.[133] Through high-quality coaching and conversation, we can begin to empower teachers to be better placed to identify their own direction of improvement. Without the distraction of data capture, student grades or influence over pay reward, this approach encourages the teacher to devote time to improving the quality of their work, with a far more fulfilling set of underpinning principles that aid their development.

Effective coaching hands over autonomy to teachers, giving them the knowledge, expertise and understanding of their own practice to begin to formulate their own goals. Coaching exposes the metacognitive processes

---

133. Pink, D. H. (2009) *Drive: The surprising truth about what motivates us.* New York: Riverhead Books.

of teaching and actively encourages the participant to continuously consider, adjust and review, strengthening their mental models for teaching so that they can more effectively identify issues in the classroom and know how to solve them.

- Effective coaching supports intrinsic motivation.
- Coaching exposes the metacognitive processes of teaching to help teachers direct their own development needs.

Utilising professional expertise and experience

Professional development focused on a 'best bets' approach to classroom delivery is increasingly informed by the cognitive and contextual evidence of our school settings. Simply put, we have limited time with students and this needs to be spent with knowledge not only of our subject, but of evidence and research that informs how that time is best spent. Tom Bennett, Founder and Director of researchED, touches upon this in his description of why researchED exists:

> It was prompted by my despair at the lack of evidence commonly used in discussions about education – from training, to teacher prep, to school strategies to political initiatives. It all seemed so haphazard and intuitive. Instead, [through researchED] practitioners could access research and academic materials quickly and easily; they could talk to and listen with one another.[134]

Subsequently, the professional development opportunities that schools provide should offer outlets for teachers to contemplate the precarious issues encountered when teaching their subject, and build upon the experiences of others to inform their own approach. Leaders of hierarchical subject disciplines can work to understand one another better, and how their subject delivery has commonality in the classroom; contrasting subjects can seek to understand that whilst the leading principles of their subjects differ, they can share teaching principles that aid learning. Nevertheless, this is not a

---

134. Kindly provided by Tom Bennett, Director and Founder of researchED.

promotion of pedagogical homogeneity; rather the acknowledgement that it is possible to learn from one another's expertise in the classroom as long as we do so with nuance and sensitivity to our subjects.

Effective professional development in action could involve discussions of how subject curriculums pay service to the structures of knowledge in each subject or the threshold concepts that underpin them, and how these have influenced sequencing and delivery. Another example could be taking a particular aspect of the subject curriculum and using short, focused discussion to outline strategies that may improve its teaching. Teachers might share and enact common issues that they have encountered within the classroom, devising two or three approaches to trial, evaluate, revisit as a group and refine. In keeping with a sense of collective vision, staff should feel involved and valued as their voices contribute to such developmental discussion.

Finally (and most importantly), when executed effectively, curriculum development should feel empowering for teaching staff. Not only does it aid the work that we do around the curriculum, but it invites staff to consider the importance of the work and where the current issues lie, and to participate without hierarchy on how best to resolve such issues.

- High-quality professional development draws on the expertise and experience of staff whilst remaining sensitive to the subject.
- Professional development should act as a means of professional empowerment.

Professional development and the subject discipline

Whilst we may look to the whole school faculty to draw on the expertise and experience we may find there, subject-based development remains the key driver of curriculum and teaching improvement. Harnessing the knowledge and expertise of subject communities; empowering staff through discourse with fellow specialists; and safeguarding time to share such experiences of what our subject discipline resembles in the classroom – these should be at the heart of teacher and curriculum development. Sterman reports:

> Individuals are more likely to improve their understanding of the systems they have created if they engage in a dialogue which tests their assumptions of causal structure of the issue.[135]

Engaging with subject communities and their discourses supports our ongoing review and refinement of our curriculum because it enables the teacher to engage with the contentious issues of their subject but without the threat or pressure of it being linked to their own performance. Quite simply, they will improve the curriculum by being part of discussions that improve the curriculum. Making time in the school schedule for professional development of this nature explicitly communicates the message that curriculum work is prioritised and valued.

Engaging with subject communities also allows teachers to spend time beyond the school walls, so they might consider how their subject looks outside of their own classroom. The focus, as always, should be on increasing opportunities for teachers to discuss the substance of the subject without the presence of accountability or judgement: *What do we teach? Why? What problems does this present to us, or our students? Which issues present themselves over and over again? Why might this be? How have we sought to work through such problems?*

Finally, collaborative planning within subject teams is one of the most powerful ways to drive professional development. The work of the curriculum is not for one or two experienced staff, but for every teacher. Experienced, expert teachers can offer their knowledge in explaining complex concepts and anticipating misconceptions, whilst novice subject specialists may offer ways to counter the effects of the curse of the expert by drawing attention to where steps may be missed or where explanations overestimate prior knowledge. These conversations strengthen the work in all of our classrooms.

---

135. Sterman, J. D. (1994) 'Learning in and about Complex Systems', *Systems Dynamics Review*, 10, 291–330.

Effective collaborative planning functions not to generate resources but to engage in meaningful discussion and deliberation of what we will teach and how best to teach it. Framing this work around questions of what will be taught at each stage of the curriculum, and undertaking this work collaboratively as a department for the week of teaching ahead, ensures focus is on supporting curriculum enactment in a way that is true to its intention and design.

- What knowledge do we plan to teach over the next week or two weeks? How can we break this down into its component parts?
- Which parts need more explicit focus than others?
- What considerations do we need to make for the types of knowledge we are teaching?
- What attention needs to be paid to threshold concepts, recontextualisation, disciplinary knowledge,[136] etc.?
- What is the core knowledge that we need to emphasise and reinforce? How will we make this 'stick'?
- What prior knowledge is required and how can we activate this?
- What misconceptions do we anticipate and how might we address them?
- Do we need to make any modifications to the curriculum and what we are teaching based on students' understanding of this unit so far? What should these look like?
- Are there any aspects of the short-term curriculum plan that we could discuss and rehearse so that we can devise a common language for our approach?
- What exemplars or models can we use to ensure students access the high standard expected?
- How can these be constructed and then broken down for students to better understand the processes involved?
- What are the best questions we can ask at this stage? What do we need to ensure students know and can articulate and how will we tease this out?

---

136. See 'Curriculum Knowledge' page 47.

We can structure collaborative planning to more precisely support teachers where needed by providing pre-tasks. For example, asking teachers to annotate their resource or the problems they will be giving to students to answer, to draw their attention to their planning process – this can be used to then discuss and deliberate over key information and methods to be used in class. Alternatively, teachers could be asked to annotate texts or sources using their current subject knowledge along with extra research in preparation for sharing this expertise in planning sessions. This more structured approach sets the standard for engagement for all teachers, both in terms of their commitment to preparing for lessons and to enhancing their subject knowledge, as well as communicating the value of their contribution by giving time to prepare and guidance to do so.

Reserving time in the calendar for iterative subject-focused discussion and planning empowers subject leads to make choices around the development of their respective teams, but also reinforces a commitment to placing ongoing curriculum development as central to all other tasks. As schools move away from one-size-fits-all, extended CPD sessions, towards a more localised, bespoke and contextualised approach for their staff, professional development sessions can then directly respond to the needs of the teachers in attendance. Even further, those teachers can then share their own expertise in the pursuit of subject-specialist cooperation, and learn from one another.

- Subject-based development remains the key driver for curriculum and teaching improvement.
- Engagement with subject communities and their discourse supports the ongoing review and refinement of the curriculum.
- Collaborative planning within subject teams is one of the most powerful ways to drive subject knowledge and effective curriculum enactment.
- Reserving time on the calendar for regular opportunities for collaborative planning communicates the value of ongoing curriculum development.

Cross-phase cooperation

In addition to spending time on subject-specific preparation to aid curriculum planning, teachers would benefit from seeking out ways to form cross-phase subject communities, in a bid to better understand the experience of students studying our subject at different ages or phases within their educational career. These conversations are essential to understanding the nuances between each of these respective phases. To what extent have teachers in a primary phase been exposed to the framework of mathematics in the preceding key stage, GCSE or beyond? What can secondary school teachers learn from the teaching of phonics and grammar in primary that will assist in the secondary classroom? What periods of history or places in geography have students already encountered and how does this prior knowledge support their current learning? For English teachers in secondary, the curriculum is often informed by the knowledge of texts studied at primary – if students have been taught *A Midsummer Night's Dream* in Year 6, to what extent can we justify its inclusion in Year 7? How might our treatment of it differ?

Equally, building these professional relationships enables us to view where our threads may fail to connect, or why students may struggle when they reach secondary school; not because of falling behind academically, but because we have not identified the differences in vocabulary employed in our subject from one phase to the next. A conjunction may have been called a connective, or the top number in a fraction may later be referred to as a numerator, and the student is taken back to the starting blocks of our subject to relearn an entirely different language. We therefore need to be mindful of these differences so that students do not get tangled in new terminology that undermines what they have previously learnt. It is increasingly important that we consider students' experience of our subjects throughout their school career, so that we can utilise this information to bridge the way across the precarious stages of each subject.

- Work to understand how students experience our subject throughout their school career.

- Make effective use of curricular time by utilising what has come before or what will come later.
- Work to understand the necessary differences between phases and why they exist.

Ambition beyond specifications

Subject knowledge is best developed when exam specifications are set aside. Whilst some colleagues might argue that a level of subject knowledge beyond the remit of a specification is superfluous, this is a flimsy rebuttal. Having a deep knowledge of our subject helps better equip us to package it for students. It is not necessary for the art teacher to have a deep understanding of Zara Hadid's spatial philosophy in order to teach Year 9 art, but it can enrich how the teacher articulates the strength and significance of visual impact, or provide insight to the way in which architecture communicates with the environment. Our knowledge of our subject should be ever-evolving and expanding, not just in our understanding of its history but of its evolution within the field. Regardless of the outline provided to us by the national curriculum or exam specification, it is our job to take students beyond this knowledge and experience, and close the gap between what they are taught in the classroom and what is being produced in our disciplinary fields. To do so requires committed engagement with the subject on behalf of the teacher and we need to offer the time, space and resources to support this.

- We need to take students beyond what is required by the national curriculum and by exam specifications.
- Investment and engagement in developing subject knowledge is key to exposing students to our subject's heritage and its current production in the field.

CHAPTER 15
EVALUATIVE DEVELOPMENT
IS CURRICULAR DEVELOPMENT

For our evaluation of curriculum to authentically support its development, we must consider how to evaluate so that the evidence is not only accurate but also valuable to our iterative journey of improvement as a profession. The CUREE 'Developing Great Leadership of CPDL' report advises that for accountability to move to a more healthy place in schools, evaluation systems should 'make it explicit to all, including in SLT, that changes to curriculum development, planning and providing support both provide great CPDL opportunities and depend on it.'[137] This dependency is most significant: if we are not evaluating in a way that supports others, and not conveying this support as essential to the journey, then the professional development and discussion intended to serve the curriculum are fruitless. As much as we need a system of evaluation that interrogates the truth of what is effective in our schools, we also need a system that values the individual and offers support, contextual understanding, honesty and investment in the process.

Being engaged with the process of teaching

If we look to visit the lessons of our teachers in the name of genuine curiosity, support and encouragement, building on what is successful and using this as an opportunity to value people and their work, then these visits serve an important purpose. If staff associate lesson visits

---

137. Cordingley, P., Higgins, S., Greany, T. et al. (2020) *Developing Great Leadership of CPDL*, accessed at http://www.curee.co.uk/files/publication/%5Bsite-timestamp%5D/Developing%20Great%20Leadership%20CPDL%20-%20final%20summary%20report.pdf.

with unease, anxiety or as measurement of their ability, then whilst our aim may be to gain an accurate snapshot to help evaluate and improve teaching, we are likely to see a performance of what a teacher perceives we want to see rather than a reflection of the students' everyday experience. The more we try to measure with checklists and scrutiny, the less accurate those measurements will be. If we look to create a culture of openness, transparency and trust in wanting everyone to improve, then our evaluations of current teaching practice are far more likely to be accurate.

Our curriculum conversations, though often informal and developmental, are also more likely to help us evaluate and triangulate where current issues lie by their very nature of being open and developmental. Such conversations are not for the purpose of catching people out but for the purpose of inquiry and honest discussion of what needs to be addressed, alongside an understanding that the subject leader's role is to support and help come to solutions for this. Such examples of this conversation might include:

- Your enquiry question asks 'Can oceans be managed sustainably?' What makes this a good question for enquiry? What knowledge would students draw upon to answer this question? How is the curriculum sequenced to support this?
- How do you decide what prior knowledge is required for this stage of learning? What connections do you ask students to make here? How does this reinforce their new learning?
- Where and how do you discuss the disciplinary aspects of your subject? What do these add to your students' understanding at each stage?
- What recurring concepts and vocabulary do your teachers use and how do you ensure students have a secure understanding of these?
- What misconceptions do you think students may have in this sequence of learning? Do all of your team know what these may be and how to pre-empt or address them?
- How do your assessments allow you to identify these misconceptions?
- Where are there opportunities for students to meaningfully apply their learning?

- At what stage would you expect students to be able to apply their learning? How far into the curriculum would this need to be for it to be meaningful?
- How has your department come to conclusions regarding the common language you will use for explaining key concepts? To what extent are these embedded in the curriculum and its enactment?
- Where have opportunities been made for meaningful interdisciplinary connections?

Such questions should not appear as interrogation or dissection of the teacher's practice, but a vested interest in the learning which takes place in the classroom as a result of the curriculum. We look to draw the teacher's attention to the process of the curriculum in action; we remove any question of the teacher's expertise, applying language that discusses the enactment of the curriculum in a way that allows for meaningful, intellectual rumination on its design and delivery. This offers space for evaluative consideration of curriculum knowledge, sequencing and delivery. It allows us to better understand the intention, implementation and impact of the curriculum in a way that moves us from these seemingly abstract terms into concrete discussion. Discussions of this nature are somewhat underestimated in schools, because they are less tangible and less high-stakes, yet they demand rigour and inquiry in a way that is far more conducive to evaluation and development. Kennedy provides valuable insight here:

> [Teachers] are likely to have formed habitual responses to students jumping out of their seats, to favor certain methods of portraying particular curriculum content, to favor certain seating arrangements, bulletin board displays, and so forth. Thus, any new idea offered by PD requires not merely adoption but also abandonment of a prior approach.[138]

---

138. Kennedy, M. (2016) 'How Does Professional Development Improve Teaching?', *Review of Educational Research*, 86.

This means the language and questions we use must act to undo values or perceptions of the past, to make way for an alternative approach. Such questions allow us to begin to evaluate the effectiveness of the curriculum, not to damage the trust and relationships that the work relies so heavily upon – but through collegiate, professional discussion of the curriculum in its current context. Colleagues don't simply listen and comply: they are active participants in discussions that communicate the value of their subject expertise and their deep understanding of the curriculum, alongside the belief that others have in their ability to improve it.

- Evaluations will be more accurate within a climate of curiosity, inquiry and development than one of high-stakes accountability.
- Conversations should place value on subject expertise and a deep understanding of the internal dynamics of the curriculum.

Questioning one thing at a time

Kennedy writes that 'from the teacher's perspective, the education system is "noisy"';[139] we often try to conduct and review too many initiatives, in response to too many voices. Systems are therefore required to encourage professional curiosity and succinct, focused feedback that does not distract teachers from the main objective or message on which we wish to focus our energies. Using enquiry for professional development involves turning data and experience into knowledge, using evidence for decision-making, participating in others' research, and promoting communities of enquiry.[140]

Adopting a curious mind for evaluation can be achieved through teacher-led inquiry projects, encouraging teachers and leaders to practise a sense of respectful objectivity to how the curriculum stands up. Leading our journey to improvement through singular lines of inquiry reduces the danger of distraction – the 'busyness' to which Kennedy alludes. Through the development of action research groups within schools – building communities that encourage teachers to address one thing at a time,

---

139. Ibid.
140. Wilkins, R. (2011) *Research Engagement for School Development*. London: Institute of Education.

informed by the evidence that presents itself not only in publications but within their classrooms in real-time – enables teachers to look for improvement of their practice instead of progress and outcomes. Evaluation of projects is not undertaken by weighing up whether the project was a success; the success is measured through the new questions posed through the journey of the project itself.

An example of an inquiry project might be: 'How can I encourage my Year 9 students to meaningfully apply the curriculum of their history lessons to the content and discussion of English?

The English teacher would then visit history lessons to understand the way in which the history curriculum is packaged and delivered; the format of the instruction; the similarities and differences of the subject disciplines; to what extent the history teacher makes explicit connections to English, and how the language or format might be replicated or adapted for their own classroom; how students are encouraged to participate in making connections between subjects; and if the wider curriculum as a whole lends itself to such an inquiry in the first place, or if further purposeful work could be done here. For the teacher, the process opens up many further questions, but they all lead back to the initial inquiry. The result of this process is the teacher's far richer understanding, which can be applied to their classroom context and used time and again, cohort to cohort, refining the process through repeated rehearsal and maintaining focused objectivity on its effectiveness throughout. This method of evaluation is measured through nothing more than the teacher engaging with the process; improvement is a natural consequence.

- Encourage professional curiosity to promote effective evaluation.
- Improve through professional inquiry.

The power of continuous critique

Much of the evaluative discussions that we have in school are difficult because the matter we are discussing is incredibly complex – we are dealing with a shared vision of curriculum but through the lens of many. Agreeing standards in advance helps establish our mental model for the gold standard of our subject. This enables discussions to reach a shared understanding far more rapidly than when conversations around curriculum open with a disparity in what we understand to be high-quality curriculum practice.

A common language when evaluating is also key to its effectiveness. Repetition and over-communication of our goals and our process to achieve them cannot be underestimated. Marzano outlines why this is paramount to our evaluation:

> Having a comprehensive model in which everybody talks about teaching in the same way communicates a message that we are serious about good teaching, we talk about teaching in this way, we expect you to think about teaching in this way and to use this model to examine your strengths and weaknesses and create a platform to allow for real reflective practice. In this way, the school or district becomes a place where you get better at teaching.[141]

These professional conversations are led by evidence and objective inquiry, and are galvanised by our established standard. These conversations should become commonplace, allowing colleagues to anticipate the analysis, guidance or support that they bring and value them as a result. These are not conversations of admin or operations; they promote a serious and deliberate evaluation in what we do, how we do it, and how we get better at it.

- Agree standards to ensure evaluation is purposeful.
- Over-communicate aims to promote a common understanding and purpose.
- Evaluation should be serious and deliberate, with the aim of working together for collective improvement.

---

141. Marzano, R. J., Waters, T. & McNulty, B. A. (2005) *School leadership that works: From research to results.* Alexandria, VA: Association for Supervision and Curriculum Development.

FINAL THOUGHTS
SYMBIOSIS: CURRICULUM
AND CLASSROOM

There is an inextricable link between our curriculum and our moral, individual and collective purpose as teachers; we need to be active participants in curricular work because it is intrinsic to our role. This important work, when done well, has the power to retain our best teachers by enabling them to remain the custodians of the curriculum, and in doing so we improve the standard of education for our students. This meaningful, academic pursuit of curriculum and subject expertise needs to be at the heart of school improvement. Through sensitive and nuanced treatment of the subject that avoids reductive genericism, alongside personalised, iterative training that equips teachers with the best bets for teaching their students, we can look to professional development that is truly catered to the teacher as a professional.

Curriculum development is central to the professional fulfilment of the teacher and the educational enrichment of the student. However, it does not have to represent more work, or insurmountable work, but instead quite the opposite – it draws a teaching community together to work on a project which offers a shared pursuit of beauty and purpose.

Through a more thoughtful and thorough understanding of what it means to develop curriculum within schools, teachers are provided with the opportunity to act as more than merely servants of curriculum. They can delve deeper into the heart of the subject itself: its internal dynamics, heritage, contentions and debates, taking them back to a nostalgic point in their own educational journey where, as a student, they first grasped the beauty of their discipline for themselves. To experience the curiosity of a novice and the pursuit of an expert is one of the most fulfilling aspects of teaching; the curriculum allows us to do just that. We cannot extricate the curriculum from those who nurture, shape and deliver it in the classroom: their relationship is symbiotic.

CPSIA information can be obtained
at www.ICGtesting.com
Printed in the USA
JSHW021920270920
8228JS00002B/5